" THE ART OF SURVEILLANCE "

By   Kelly E. Riddle

Copyright 2013
By
Kelly E. Riddle

All rights reserved. No part of this publication may be reproduced or transmitted in any form or by any means, electronic or mechanical, including photocopy, recording, or any information storage and retrieval system, without permission in writing from the author, except for brief excerpts for reviews.

Published by
Kelly E. Riddle
2553 Jackson Keller, Suite 200
San Antonio, TX. 78230
(210) 342-0509

TABLE OF CONTENTS

Chapter One: Introduction	Page 4
Chapter Two: Surveillance Equipment	Page 11
Chapter Three: What People Don't Talk About	Page 19
Chapter Four: Foot Surveillance	Page 22
Chapter Five: Vehicle/Mobile Surveillance	Page 35
Chapter Six: Other Types of Surveillance	Page 65
Chapter Seven: Stationary Surveillance	Page 73
Chapter Eight: Face-To-Face Contact	Page 84
Chapter Nine: Out-Sourcing Investigations	Page 92
Chapter Ten: Writing the Report	Page 97
Chapter Eleven: Marketing Your Services	Page 105
Chapter Twelve: Legalities of Surveillance	Page 109
Chapter Thirteen: So You Want to Be a PI	Page 118
Chapter Fourteen: Counter Surveillance	Page 134
Chapter Fifteen: GPS and Drones	Page 144
Chapter Sixteen: International Surveillance	Page 155
Chapter Seventeen: About the Author	Page 169
Index	Page 171

INTRODUCTION TO SURVEILLANCE
Chapter One

Surveillance is simply "discovering" without being discovered. The whole idea of surveillance is to obtain information and documentation that can't be obtained any other way. This doesn't mean that investigators break the law to accomplish this. It simply means that the person's activities can't be properly documented by checking records and doing typical background investigations. Surveillance is done for a variety of reasons, at the request of a variety of people using a variety of techniques. For instance, the government has "spies" who conduct surveillance in other countries to determine the activities and potential threat of a person or organization to the United States. Law enforcement officials conduct surveillance and "sting" operations to document criminal behavior. Private industries conduct surveillance to determine what their competitors are up to and to protect trade secrets. Then there is the average person who may want to determine if their spouse is being unfaithful. Each of these examples has the opportunity to succeed or to create negative publicity and situations.

Surveillance is not a game, even though I have often heard it referred to as a "cat and mouse game". In the instances above, if other countries catch a U.S. spy, the potential for an international incident escalates. If an investigator for a corporation is discovered, the company runs the risk of poor publicity, lawsuits, and damage to their reputation and financial losses. Although an investigator conducting surveillance in a domestic case doesn't typically run the risks that these others do, the investigator's reputation may be jeopardized and claims against them and their insurance carrier may arise. It is therefore extremely important that a person understand the risks to themselves and their client before they undertake surveillance.

Due to the increase of stalking related crimes, most States now have laws to protect the public from stalking. My experiences have shown that most of these laws require a person to report the situation to the police at least three times before the "stalker" can be charged under these laws. This law alone, if for no other reason, should cause the untrained and unlicensed person to think twice before conducting surveillance themselves. In addition, most States have regulatory boards that over-see licensing requirements and provide for criminal and civil punishment if in violation of these regulations. With these things in mind, the "average" person should refrain from conducting surveillance themselves and request those individuals who are properly licensed and trained to handle the situation.

The *art* of surveillance is an acquired skill that relies on the investigator's own instincts, as well as learned techniques. Because of the nature of the job, it can be as dangerous as the investigator makes it. If the right equipment and techniques are utilized, the subject should never be aware that surveillance is being conducted. On the other hand, if the investigator is not properly trained, does not have proper equipment and gets too comfortable during the investigation, a confrontation with the subject being followed may be the end result. Sometimes, the person being investigated is just naturally suspicious and even the most experienced investigators have difficulty with these. I conducted surveillance at times when I discovered that there are other investigators watching the same subject because he had more than one insurance claim or the police department's vice squad was interested in the subject. Surveillance is not only observing the behavior of the subject in question, but those around you as well. In these types of situations where more than one investigator is involved, if I hadn't observed the movements of the other investigators that lead me to discover their identities, we may have blown the cases for all of the investigators involved.

Although certain basic skills can be taught to a potential investigator, the success of the investigation is often determined by the natural instincts of the investigator. You can't teach someone when they should discontinue surveillance because the investigation is in jeopardy or how to react the right way in difficult situations. Unfortunately, T.V. tends to portray surveillance in a way that makes most people believe that it is easy and that they can do it.

What I have found through my years of experience is that approximately only two out of five potential investigators are right for the job. Sometimes, it is the potential investigator that finds out that the reality of the job is not what they had thought and they decide not to pursue this career. Surveillance tends to be one of those jobs where there is very little going on, and therefore tends to be boring, or there is a lot happening and your adrenaline is going full-force. When you add hot or cold temperatures, rain, snow, having to use the bathroom at the most inopportune times and similar factors, one can easily see how this is not a job for everyone.

Some of the earliest uses of surveillance, or "spying" can be traced back to Biblical times as noted in Deuteronomy 1:22. The twelve tribes of Israel had been wandering the desert for forty-years, waiting on the land that God had promised to give them as their own. As they approached the land, the text indicates "Then all of you came to me and said, Let us send men ahead to spy out the land for us and bring back a report about the route we are to take and the towns we will come to." Armies used surveillance to document the movement of the enemy, to determine the strength of their foes, the type of weapons they had and the tactics they were most likely to use. This has long sense escalated to high-tech surveillance using satellites and "spy" aircraft that take photographs of the terrain.

Surveillance, in its strictest form, is even used today by coaches who "scout" their opponents. They conduct surveillance as a means of determining the strengths, weaknesses, best players and the types of plays their opponents use. The art of surveillance is even developed as kids by playing games like "hide and seek". The children develop their skills by having to conduct "surveillance" of the area to locate and pick out the movements of their opponents. Surveillance, in fact, can even be listed as an instinct developed by nature in the struggle for survival in the strongest of the strong contest. Lions and other animals have developed the ability to conduct "surveillance" on their potential prey to observe their movements that will allow them to out-smart the prey. So, surveillance, although it often has a negative connotation, is a primal instinct that has been developed into a useful tool.

The increase in technology has prompted the art of surveillance to change and become more high-tech as well. Surveillance has gone from simply "scouting" out a situation, to having to adjust to movement due to horses, boats, ships, trains, bicycles, cars, vans, motorcycles, airplanes and everything in between. What once was merely using the naked eye to observe, has grown into a billion dollar industry of supplying "spy" equipment for the government, law enforcement officials, private investigations, private industry and even criminals.

Unfortunately, whatever is used against criminals is almost always used on behalf of criminals. Take for example, stagecoach robberies. The outlaws had to conduct surveillance on the stagecoach route to determine the routes, times and the best place to ambush the stage. In modern day use, criminals are known to use high-tech infrared night vision devices to see movement of law enforcement officials before they can be detected themselves. More like the stagecoach approach are those documented cases in which criminals have conducted surveillance on an armored car that ultimately leads to an ambush and theft of the contents. Then there is computer "spying" which is now known as hacking. A computer can have the contents broken into, spied on and information copied, altered or destroyed.

The increase in technology has also helped develop surveillance into an industry. In earlier forms, the investigator was required to testify as to what they observed, and at best, supply witnesses to back up his story. Today, the use of video cameras, long range zoom lenses, hidden cameras, infra-red night vision units, computers, VCR's, DVR's, TV's, still photographs from video, computer enhanced photos and a variety of other devices makes "a picture worth a thousand words" take on more meaning. Even though investigators are often called upon to testify in court or in a deposition, the questions usually have to do with the methods used to obtain the video and the "chain of custody" in which the evidence was secured. Since the photographic documentation methods have dramatically improved, most insurance companies, attorneys, corporations and individuals now feel more comfortable using surveillance, as they will be able to see for themselves what results were obtained. No longer do they have to make decisions solely on the testimony of an investigator.

The use of good, professional surveillances has been a tremendous method of self-marketing for the industry. As more and more court battles are won based on good surveillance techniques, properly written reports and excellent video documentation, the use of surveillance has also increased.

The methods of surveillance are typically stationary and non-stationary and an investigation may begin with one and end up crossing back and forth between the two. It is not uncommon for a stationary surveillance unit to have to become mobile once the targeted subject leaves a particular location. If you initiate surveillance at a person's home where you are stationary, the target may exit the house, put fishing gear in the car and travel to the beach where they get into a boat. Your ability to adapt to these situations is critical to the success of the investigation. Some of the surveillance methods include vehicle surveillance, closed-circuit camera surveillance, foot/pedestrian surveillance, boat, ship, airplane, bicycle, motorcycle, train, subway, horse, commercial vehicle (bus, 18-wheeler) and similar areas of surveillance. The bottom line is that the investigator has to be ready to change positions, methods and pre-set mental ideas to adapt to the environment.

The use of more than one investigator can aid in the success of the investigation if they have the right equipment and talents. If you have five investigators on the same surveillance, but they do not have communications or are improperly prepared, there might as well only be one investigator there. Law Enforcement related surveillances usually are fortunate to have both the equipment and the manpower. However, I have seen times when even these types of investigators have more than they can handle and are forced to work with only one or two investigators. Private investigators, on the other hand, are somewhat limited in manpower by several factors, which include the client's ability and willingness to pay for more than one investigator. In addition, PI's tend to be improperly staffed and often resort to part-time help who are not adequately trained. The professional PI is usually ready for fluctuations in manpower needs and has invested enough capital into purchasing the right equipment for the job. Poorly equipped investigators are often an indication that they only do that type of work on a part-time basis or are under-capitalized and may not be in business too long anyway.

The need, desire and acceptance of surveillance have never been greater than in recent years. With popular T.V. talk shows spending hours of broadcasts showing corruption, insurance fraud, theft, domestic problems and similar situations, the public has become more aware of surveillance. Almost every person who pays insurance understands the need for surveillance when a jury awards millions of dollars to a person and then sees video documentation of the subject jumping out of the wheelchair after winning the case.

Corporations are also seeing the increased need for surveillance because of internal employee theft, accidents and costly liability issues. Retail stores are finding that not only do video cameras of the shopping area help deter external theft, it also helps to confirm or contradict slip and fall injuries to patrons, misconduct of employees and provides marketing information as to which displays seem to catch a shopper's eye the most. Internal theft in all businesses has been a source of concern and they have attempted to combat this through the use of surveillance equipment. Several cases have recently been decided which set the boundaries of privacy for employees at the workplace. However, with this being a tool that is becoming more and more widely used by businesses, a form of checks and balances were bound to arise.

Individuals are finding the need for surveillance as well. The use of this tool to determine whether a spouse or potential spouse is untruthful seems to be on the increase. An investigator must especially be aware of the legal boundaries surrounding this type of surveillance as illegal intrusions may lead to civil and criminal penalties. Besides the common "unfaithful spouse" cases, individuals are now turning to surveillance to document the activity of their children. The hopes of the parents are that if they can prove to themselves and their children that the child has an alcohol or drug problem, they can get them counseling before the police get involved or they further jeopardize their life. Surveillance appears to be just the tool parents are clinging to in these types of situations. Pre-marital investigations are also showing an increase in surveillance use, as the potential spouses want to determine if the subject's activities are consistent with their life style. Through surveillance, they are able to confirm other relationships, the way the subject handles their finances (shops a lot, etc.), appears to be in debt (owns a house, boat, lake house, etc.) or has criminal tendencies such as selling drugs.

Closed Circuit TV (CCTV) cameras are more and more prevalent as a normal tool in society. Highways and roadways have cameras watching activity, police departments are using cameras stationed in high-population areas such as downtown locations to monitor traffic and criminal activity and the average person has cell phones completed with video capabilities. The world as a whole has become more acceptable to cameras due to terrorist threats. In Britain for example, there are up to 4.2 million CCTV cameras (about one for every 14 people).[1]

Surveillance has become a more widely used and accepted type of investigation, although it is usually far from the way T.V. portrays it. The need in every sector of our society appears to be on the increase and a properly trained PI with the right equipment stands to do quite well in this area in the years ahead. Most insurance companies and large corporations have staff investigators who conduct the background investigations themselves, but assign the surveillances to an outside contractor. Therefore, from all indications, surveillance is here to stay and will be one of the tools that PI's use to profit by in the future.

---

[1] http://news.bbc.co.uk/2/hi/uk_news/6108496.stm

SURVEILLANCE EQUIPMENT
Chapter Two

The equipment that the investigator has or does not have will dramatically affect the outcome of the surveillance. Some of the equipment can be fairly expensive, while most of the tools are off the shelf items that can be competitively shopped for the best prices. Asking an investigator to conduct surveillance without the right equipment is about like asking a fireman to put out a building fire with a water pistol. The set up can be as expensive and lavish as the investigator desires, but the bottom line is that it has to work. The investigator has to know that the surveillance vehicle or location provides them with the best concealment possible. Without this sense of confidence, the investigator will always be concerned about who can detect them and not pay appropriate attention to the target. Once the concealment is not a concern, the camera and equipment has to function properly. Using old cameras in need of cleaning and maintenance are a disaster waiting to happen. The investigator then needs to have quick access to items like long-range zoom lenses, radios, cellular telephones, computers and related equipment.

The method of surveillance will greatly determine the types and amount of equipment you will have available to you. If you are conducting surveillance on foot, carrying a lot of equipment is not practical and may be a "give-away" to the target that you are an investigator. While in your vehicle, you have the availability to carry more equipment. Some of the items that are an absolute must for an investigator include:

1. Binoculars
2. Video camera
3. Battery packs, D.C. power converter
4. Communications
5. Sunshades, window tint, etc...
6. 35 mm digital camera
7. Back-up memory cards
8. Additional concealment items

The obvious need for a good set of binoculars almost goes

without saying. Being able to zoom in on a license plate, a person's face or other characteristics is essential. There are a tremendous amount of binoculars on the market starting at about $19.00 and going up from there. The cost and size of the binoculars really comes down to the investigator's preference. A good, sturdy pair, regardless of the price is the main intent in purchasing this item. Some are more sensitive to low-light conditions and may therefore be of particular use in some cases. I have found that binoculars are usually clearer and easier to handle than a camera with a zoom lens on it and are therefore better for identification purposes.

The type of video camera that you use is somewhat dependent on prices and types available. However, standard off the shelf cameras are appropriate for this line of work. They are small, concealable and record to their internal hard-drive and/or a memory card. Periodic cleaning of the camera should be a regular requirement. Another consideration when purchasing additional cameras should be to purchase the same name brand because all of the adapters and optional equipment will interchange.

An investigator should not rely on the battery packs that come with the cameras for power because the life of these batteries will not last under the continual use and difference in temperatures that they will be subjected to. I can tell you that there aren't many things worse than not having a functioning camera when you need one. There are cigarette lighter adapters (DC) that allow you to power the camera off of the vehicle's battery or off of a larger battery pack. The cigarette lighter adapters usually cost from $30-60 and can be purchased at most camera shops. A DC to AC adapter can also be purchased which allows you to plug normal male ended plugs into female outlets which has power converted from the vehicle's battery into normal AC power. This may be useful if you want to run additional equipment. However, I would still have a cigarette lighter adapter to connect to a larger battery when you have to be out of the vehicle. Most camera shops also sale large DC power packs that provide 5-6 hours of use and are typically around $65.00 each.

Additional video camera lenses can be purchased to enhance the capabilities of the factory lens. There are "doublers" which doubles the power of the existing lens and then there are more powerful types that increase the power of the existing lens 3-12 times. Things to consider when purchasing these additional lenses are the weight, low-light capabilities and grainy characteristics. Normally, the bigger the zoom lens the more light required or they will have a grainy appearance when fully zoomed. If the lens is heavy, but does not come with a brace or support to help stabilize the unit, the weight may cause undue stress on the frame of the camera and cause damage. The technology of the over-the-counter cameras are increasing dramatically and additional lenses may quickly become a thing of the past.

An investigator should also invest in a good 35 mm digital camera that can be used to get close-up facial photographs of the subject for identification. In addition, this can be used for taking photographs of accident scenes, vehicle damage and similar uses. The digital format allows you the opportunity to import and export the video to allow to copy into reports and resize as needed. Obviously, the investigator will need at least one DVD/VCR and a TV for reviewing and copying video.

The investigator should also keep additional blank memory cards with them so that the cards can be switched out in cases where an extensive amount of video is obtained. There should also be a "master" copy kept at the investigator's office in case the client loses the first copy.

Communication equipment needs largely depend on the number of investigators that are employed. Radio communications are a necessity if you have more than two investigators employed as relying on cellular phones runs up high bills and the transmissions are easily intercepted. I have seen investigators who use C.B. radios, which is not a good idea for security reasons and due to a lack of range. There is UHF radio systems available that generally allow you to cover a 40-50 mile radius, but are commonly a shared channel with other businesses. Again, you have a security problem with this and also have to wait your turn to use the radio. The VHF radio systems are the best all-around systems as they are the same used by police agencies. They are good for security as they are a private channel and they generally cover a 50-90 mile radius using repeaters mounted on towers throughout the area. Having two or more investigators conducting surveillance on the same case without communications is ridiculous and not cost-effective to the client. When this happens, one investigator usually ends up following the other around due to not having the ability to properly communicate.

The vehicle concealment capabilities are one of the more important issues that will "make or break" an investigator. If the vehicle is prepared so that people can't see inside the vehicle, the investigator feels more confident and is therefore more effective. Depending on the laws of the particular State, dark window tinting can typically be applied to assist in this. However, in some States, the driver and passenger windows have to have a lighter shade of tint. There are several ways of making these more concealed which include the window pull-down shades that usually have small see through holes in them. I have found that you can cut Plexiglas in the shape of the glass, making it just slightly smaller. You can then put dark tint on this and insert these against the windows while sitting still and remove them when driving. This still allows you to see without being seen. An investigator should also invest in the cardboard type front window shades. These should be very plain to prevent attention being drawn to them and several extras should be carried in cases of extensive surveillance where the subject is followed to numerous locations. The shades can be switched out to make it appear like a different vehicle.

I have spoken to just about every investigator I know about what type of vehicle they like the best for surveillance. This is a topic that can be beat to death if not careful. You generally have those investigators who think the only way to conduct surveillance is by using a van. Then there are those who wouldn't use a van even if you gave them one. The consensus seems to be that all investigators would *like* to use a van, but the average citizen *expects* a PI to be in a van. I would *like* to use an R.V., but you have to be able to adapt and these types of R.V. and vans just don't get the job done. A van is hard to "blend" in where, as other vehicles are less conspicuous.

I know of one Federal investigator that is issued a van with every available piece of equipment you can think of in it. The investigator has been at it more than 15 years and I have seen him in action. The guy knows what he is doing, but he is constantly getting made because of the van. He should just hang a sign outside indicating an investigator is inside because everyone else knows he is there.

Don't get me wrong, there is a time and a place for everything, but on a day-to-day basis, vans are lacking. The bottom line on this topic comes down to the individual investigator's preference and their financial ability.

For additional concealment, the investigator should have a curtain rod that hangs directly behind the front seats with curtains that can be pushed open and then closed easily. These help to block out the limited light that still gets through the tint. Clothing is another area that attention should be given. Dark clothes should be worn whenever possible to make it even more difficult for someone to see inside.

All equipment should be properly maintained and this tends to be an area that is overlooked due to hectic schedules. The investigator should make sure that their vehicle is ready for surveillance which includes clean windows, water in the radiator, oil in the engine, proper air pressure in the tires and a full tank of gas. If you are conducting surveillance on a subject who is very active and you do not have enough gasoline to follow the subject, it could get embarrassing when you are forced to drop the surveillance to get gasoline. The cleaner the windows, the clearer the video and the least amount of haze. The investigator would be wise to carry a rag and window cleaner with them in their vehicle for just this type of situation.

There are several items that are somewhat optional, at least until you need them. During surveillance, it is not uncommon to follow the subject to a gym, office building, bar or similar situation. Depending on the reason for the surveillance, it may necessitate getting video of the subject inside these areas. For example, if you are working a case involving an alleged injury, it would be important to get video of a subject lifting weights at a gym. If you were asked to follow a person regarding a domestic case to see if they are unfaithful, getting video of the subject inside a bar would be beneficial. However, walking in with a video in your hand would draw too much attention and the employees may not allow you to enter with the camera. Therefore, an investigator should consider having a large gym bag ready for concealing a camera. There are several ways to do this that includes choosing a bag with mesh netting on the side and poking small holes through the canvass. The camera can then be situated to shoot video out of the small holes and the holes in the mesh netting will conceal the other holes. One of the best differences between a 35 mm digital camera and a video camera is that a 35 mm camera has to have the entire lens clear of any obstructions. A video camera, on the other hand, requires sufficient light and can obtain clear video through numerous small holes or even a single hole.

The technology relating to video cameras is increasing rapidly. Many either record to a small digital video recorder (DVR) or to a memory card. Some of the items out on the market that have hidden video cameras in them are smoke detectors, exit signs, lamps, pagers, pens, tie clips and other related items. In addition to these, there are small helium types balloons (similar to those used by T.V. stations for professional football games) that are remote controlled and have a video camera with zoom capabilities. These currently start around $5,000.

Another method of obtaining video is through the use of remote control airplanes, helicopters, boats and submarines. Because camera lenses are continually being updated and the ability to have a wireless camera that work at greater ranges are increasing, the use of these items will be sure to increase as well.

There are briefcases with video cameras hidden in them that can be purchased starting at about $1,000. However, if you can find a wide enough briefcase that will allow you to close the top with a camera in it, you can design your own for less money. Position the camera in the briefcase and use a pencil to mark where the camera lens hits the inside of the case. Take a small drill bit and drill holes in a circle to coincide with the camera lens. Afterwards, take some shoe polish and dab the holes to make them blend in with the color of the briefcase.

A good, lightweight tri-pod should also be obtained for those situations when you are forced to be out of your vehicle in a field or similar situation. Placing the camera on the tri-pod will allow you to keep the camera steady and will not tire you out trying to hold it. In these types of situations, it would be advisable to have a hand held radio for communicating with other investigators when you're out of the vehicle. Incidentally, the investigator should remember to turn their pager to "vibration" and to turn the radio or cellular telephones to the lowest volume level because sound travels a great distance. Even if a person can't hear them, a dog may hear the noise and come to investigate!

One of the often over-looked areas of video is how to make copies and keep the time/date stamp on the video when you make a copy. Most video cameras will not transfer the time/date stamp rending the video virtually useless for the client. There are several ways of handling this.

Pinnacle Studio

The software program, Pinnacle Studio is like any other program that you load onto your computer. The full version comes with a docking station for you to plug your video camera in and this is critical to capturing your time/date stamp. This program is large and requires 4.5 GB HDD space for installation. It is designed for making professional movies and has all of the editing features. The biggest drawback is the time it takes to copy your video onto your computer.

Sony DVD burner:

Pictured below, the Sony DVD burner allows the video camera to be plugged directly into the unit or you can insert various sizes of memory cards into the slots on the burner.

The Sony DVD burner pictured above is one of the easiest and cost effective methods for transferring video while keeping the time and date stamp.

For private investigators, good sources of surveillance equipment include:

1) The Spy Exchange in Austin, TX. - http://www.pimall.com/nais/equ.find.html

2) Inet Security & Surveillance in San Antonio, TX - http://inetsas.com/

3) The Spy Store in Spokane, WA - http://thespystore.com/

4) Spy Gear Gadgets in Henderson, TN - http://www.spygeargadgets.com/

An investigator without the minimum professional equipment will soon be out of business. There is too much competition and professional investigators easily stand out from the rest of the pack.

WHAT PEOPLE DON'T TALK ABOUT
Chapter Three

Investigators are often taught the functional aspect of surveillance but few ever discuss mistakes. Although mistakes, by very definition are "an error in action, calculation, opinion, or judgment caused by poor reasoning, carelessness, insufficient knowledge, etc.[2] they can also create a lot of problems for you as well as your relationship with your client. However, many of these errors can be minimalized or completely prevented if the proper care is taken from the beginning.

Failure to Prepare - Research

Often the investigator does not take the proper time to evaluate the street, neighborhood and general location for good surveillance locations prior to leaving for the actual surveillance. Even if the PI knows the neighborhood, streets can be altered or added so verification will prevent the person from slipping out the newly created street at the back of the neighborhood. With Google Earth, you can get a good idea of the area via the Internet.

Even if your client does not pay for a background report, you owe it to yourself to run a complete background to make sure you are not watching someone who recently got out of jail for murder and could possibly have violent tendencies. Additionally you should confirm if they actually are still reporting that address or if they have a more current one listed. While doing the research, confirm the vehicles registered to them and the address as well as verifying any license plates provided.

Equipment Preparation

Anything that is shinny and reflects light should be reviewed to insure this does not give up your concealment. When possible, buy black equipment and if needed, use black spray to cover reflective

---
[2] http://dictionary.reference.com/browse/mistake?s=t

areas. If the camera has a red LED light that indicates it is in the record function, spray paint this or cover with black electrical tape.

Using a laptop on surveillance, a video game, cell phone or anything else that omits light may cause what appears to be an unoccupied vehicle to become a sudden give-away of your concealment. Radio sound inside of your vehicle may also be too loud and cause attention to be drawn to a previously ignored parked car. A good rule of thumb is to turn your radio volume up to the level you normally keep it during surveillance. Get out of the vehicle and walk away and see how far a person would have to be before they hear the radio. The same should be done for video, laptop or any other piece of equipment that omits light. This should be done both during the day and at night. Adjustments should be made in your use of this equipment based on these tests. Of course many people now use IPod's, ear-buds and other listening devices. While this may eliminate sound being omitted, it also may restrict what you hear and thus restrict useful information gathering during the course of the investigation.

The interior dome light of a vehicle normally comes on automatically when the door is opened. If trying to sneak out of the car to follow someone on foot, this could illuminate your presence unnecessarily. To prevent this, you can remove the bulb from the light or remove the fuse from the fuse box as long as the fuse does not make other gauges or lights inoperable.

A useful device for surveillance is a "kill" switch for the ignition. When operational, the kill switch prevents the engine from running while allowing the car to sound like it is attempting to crank.[3] This is useful in those cases, particularly in rural areas where you need to get video of a subject but there is no place to blend in. You can fake car trouble and continue with obtaining video. Once you obtain the needed video, simply shut the hood, throw the kill switch and the engine becomes operational again.

<u>Accessories</u>

---

[3] http://www.ehow.com/how_7995850_make-kill-switch-cars.html

Many people like bumper stickers, antenna ornaments, decorative lights and special rims and tires. On an investigator's vehicle these are an absolute "no". When following people, these make the vehicle easier to spot from a distance. As a PI, it makes the person pay attention to your vehicle and simply is a mistake.

Smoking

For those investigators that smoke cigarettes, caution should be taken to prevent smoke billowing out of a cracked window. Additionally anyone walking could also smell the cigarette smoke and once again be the source of giving up your concealment.

A person conducting surveillance can get into routines, both good and bad. If you get lulled into a sense of repetition, mistakes are most likely to happen. You fail to check your equipment, fail to think about your surroundings and eventually stop thinking about the case. You fill your time with magazines, a book or something else to occupy your non-active time. The next thing you know, you look up and the car is gone. If the person you are surveilling maintains schedules and routines, this makes the PI's job easier. Even so, people deviate. Prepare, stay alert and maintain good fundamental preparation skills!

THE BASICS OF FOOT SURVEILLANCE
Chapter Four

Foot surveillance can be one of the most difficult types of surveillance, regardless of how many investigators you are using. It is not uncommon to follow a subject to a bus stop where they catch a bus downtown. If you are in a vehicle, the first problem becomes finding a quick place to park when the subject exits the bus. The next problem is trying to quickly get your equipment together, placing it in a concealed bag and then having to tote the equipment all over downtown. If a person is not walking downtown but is walking or jogging in a neighborhood, these pose other problems. You have to position your vehicle ahead of the subject to shoot video of the subject coming towards you and then passing you. This is not usually a problem, until the subject keeps seeing you doing a "leap-frog". Usually to avoid suspicions, remaining behind the subject and shooting video from the back allows you to remain less conspicuous. Keep in mind that you still have to get good facial recognition video footage for identification purposes.

People are subject to go to all kinds of places that could present problems for the investigator who is called upon to conduct foot surveillance. Some of these places include flea markets, shopping malls, rodeo performances, picnics, parks, and theme parks like Sea World or Six Flags, office complexes, schools and universities and anyplace else people tend to go. A good investigator will use the natural tendencies of human beings to their advantage in these types of situations. For example, if you are following someone on the lower level in a shopping mall, the best place for surveillance is on the level above them.

People have a natural tendency to not look up. If you stay above them and slightly behind the subject, this should not be a problem. The investigator has to learn to use natural concealment without being obvious. For example, if following a subject on the same level in a shopping mall, the investigator should attempt to walk so that free standing signs, booths, poles and people are in between the subject and the investigator. In this way, if the subject looks back or decides to turn around, one step to the left or right will place the investigator behind a sign or other obstruction. Even if the investigator is 10-15 feet from the sign, placing the obstruction in the line of sight of the subject will help maintain the investigator's concealment. Surveillance in malls is more prominent because most malls now encourage people to walk in the malls for exercise as well as to shop.

Theme parks, neighborhood parks and schools tend to not be quite as difficult to conduct foot surveillance. This is primarily due to the fact that video cameras are fairly common at these locations. Being able to blend into the crowd and shoot video makes this type of situation much easier. One of the tricks in this type of situation is to position yourself across from the subject and far enough away so that they will not immediately observe you when the subject looks in your direction. You can create enough distance so the person will focus on other pedestrians when they glance up. This is perfect at a zoo, theme park, flea market or related places. The most difficult part of these types of cases is continually being in the same area as the subject without being too close. It can get very uncomfortable if you and the subject continue to meet face to face throughout the park.

Common techniques when following subjects on foot include walking on the opposite side of the street and behind the subject. This way, if they change direction and cross-over, you are already behind them and do not attract attention mimicking their actions.

You can also act like you need to tie your shoe, pick up the keys you intentionally dropped, or stop to buy a pack of gum or newspaper from a street vendor. All of these give you the appearance of normal activity that would be associated with a pedestrian walking down the street.

Other techniques include turning the corner differently than the subject. For example:

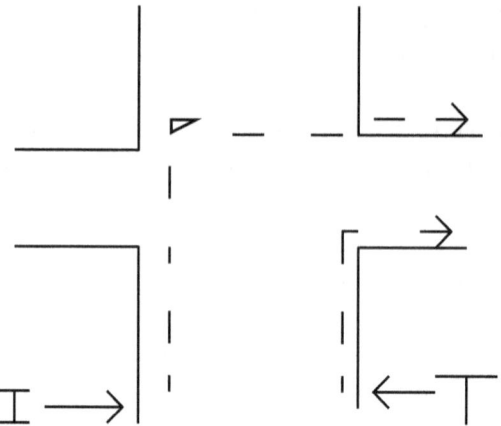

In this situation, the investigator (I) is on the left side of the street and the target (T) is on the right side. As the target approaches the corner and turns right, the investigator should attempt to cross the street going straight ahead, cross at the next intersection and continue following the target on the opposite side of the street. Several factors determine how the investigator handles foot surveillance in this type of situation including the amount of vehicle traffic, the amount of other pedestrian traffic and the light conditions. If it is dark outside and there are low light conditions, the investigator may not have the luxury of this type of surveillance and may therefore have to stay close behind the target. The investigator normally should try to keep sufficient distance between themselves and the subject so that if the target stops, turns around or changes directions the investigator can adjust as well without drawing attention.

A good investigator always keeps a "jump bag" of items that can assist in ever-changing environments. If it becomes apparent that you will be following someone on foot, dress in layers, stick a couple of baseball hats in the coat pocket along with a change of sunglasses. If the person walks around the corner or in a large crowd, take advantage and put on a hat and take off the jacket. In the summer, take off the button down shirt to reveal a t-shirt.

The investigator should always continue to scan the street with their eyes, looking for obstacles to avoid, signs to hide behind, benches to sit on, animals to pet, cars to admire or any changes in the environment. All of the senses need to be utilized. Smells can tell you of upcoming water fountains, a nearby bakery, lawn cuttings or similar bits of information. Listening to the sounds can also tell you of an approaching emergency vehicle, tires screeching, doors slamming, hastening footsteps, basketballs bouncing and a host of sensory activity.

While "war stories" are entertaining, I only try to use them for teaching or enforcement purposes. As such, one case that I worked placed all of these techniques to the test when a client requested our agency to investigate a problem employee. This particular employee was suspected as having a drug and alcohol problem, poor work quality and had abused his sick leave. The client had found out that the subject, who worked in one of their field offices in West Texas, was going to call in sick even though he did not have any sick days, emergency leave or vacation time left. Their information indicated that he was going to tell his supervisor that he had to attend the funeral of an Uncle just across the border in Mexico. However, he was supposed to drive to San Antonio where he was going to board an airplane and travel to Arizona where he was to spend the weekend with a female employee in the same company. Both subjects were married to other people and were apparently having an extra-marital affair. The client had indicated they had intended to terminate the employee for poor work performance. If he did in fact go through with the trip, the client intended on terminating him for abuse of their sick leave policy. The client was concerned about a wrongful termination lawsuit and therefore asked our agency to follow the subject and document his activities over the weekend in question.

Our agency immediately began a background investigation that confirmed the subject had been arrested for drug and alcohol related offenses. Information also revealed his having domestic arguments that required police intervention. Sources provided information indicating he was suspected as trading in stolen property and drugs.

The price of this investigation was virtually of non-importance to our client and therefore we used three investigators. On the day in question, the client confirmed the subject did in fact call in with a family emergency indicating he would not be at work on Thursday or Friday. Through various contacts and sources, we were able to confirm the subject had reservations on a flight to Arizona. We arranged to have an investigator sit in the seat near the subject in hopes of overhearing any conversations that would divulge some of his plans. After talking with the client, we immediately set the plan into action by sending one investigator ahead to Arizona on an earlier flight. This investigator did the preliminary work of scouting the airport layout, making vehicle arrangements and preparing for the arrival of the subject.

Two additional investigators stationed themselves near the ticket counter at the airport more than an hour ahead of the posted flight time. One of these investigators checked in with the ticket personnel and confirmed their seating arrangement. About thirty minutes before the flight was scheduled to leave, a subject believed to be the target arrived at the ticket counter, spoke briefly and proceeded to the nearby bar. Our investigators had been given a description of the subject but no photograph was available. Surveillance of the ticket area and the bar now had to be conducted. Fortunately, the investigators had video cameras concealed in briefcases, which allowed for easier documentation. Our client wanted video of the subject actually getting on the airplane, video of the ticket counter sign advertising the flight and video of the subject exiting the airplane in Arizona with video indicating it was Arizona.

The boarding call was announced and one investigator boarded the airplane and took his designated seat. The subject was not on board, or at least not in his designated seat. The final boarding call was issued and the third investigator told the ticket clerk that he thought the man sitting in the bar with the black cowboy hat on was supposed to be on board the flight. The clerk radioed the personnel closing the airplane door and asked them to hold the airplane. The clerk sprinted down to the bar and got the subject, who turned out to be the target. Thankfully, the subject was on his way to being intoxicated and didn't stop to think how the ticket clerk knew he was suppose to be on the airplane. The ground crew had already shut the door to the airplane, but they agreed to open it and let the subject on board. We left the third investigator in San Antonio and now had one investigator in Arizona and one on the airplane with the target.

Once the subject got onto the airplane, he took the first seat available and did not sit in his designated seat dear the investigator. The opportunity to converse with a half intoxicated subject for the duration of the flight was too tempting, so the investigator waited for just the right moment and then moved to a seat near the subject where he could at least over-hear his conversations. Once the airplane left, the investigator in San Antonio called the investigator in Arizona and confirmed that the subject was on board. The airport they would be flying into had been scouted and found to present some problems because people can drive around the terminal in a circle. This means that the female subject could pick-up the target on either side of the building and now posed a new logistical problem.

As the airplane was scheduled to arrive the investigator in Arizona parked the car in the only available spot close to the exit doors, which was a fire-lane. This would give the investigator 10-15 minutes before the airport police became concerned with the vehicle (pre 9-1-1). The investigator parked the car and then hurried to the arrival gate just as the airplane was taxing to the gate. The investigator once again had a video camera in a briefcase and had spotted the female subject believed to be meeting the target. As the doors to the airplane opened, the target was about the tenth person out and he proceeded straight into the arms of the female. They embraced and began to kiss and hold her. Of course, video was obtained of this and the surroundings that would document the location. The second investigator came off the airplane and met the first investigator. Both were carrying hand-held radios inside their jackets for communication purposes. Instead of the subjects heading towards the baggage area they walked to a nearby bar.

One investigator conducted surveillance at the bar while the other went to move the car from the fire lane and park it in the adjoining parking deck. Just as the investigator got back to the bar, the subjects decided to leave. The investigator then hurried back to the car, left the parking deck and waited patiently for the subjects while not knowing where they would exit. The second investigator followed the couple to the baggage area where the target retrieved his luggage. The couple then entered an elevator with only the investigator being the only other person in the elevator. Suddenly voices started coming out of the investigator's jacket (hand-held radio)! The investigator was able to convince them that he had a portable AM/FM radio that he forgot to turn down. The couple was so involved with each other; they didn't think anything about it!

The couple exited the elevator and entered the parking deck where it became obvious that the female subject had no idea where her car was parked. This made for a difficult time as the couple would stop, look around, change directions all of a sudden and make irrational movements. When the couple finally found their car, they sat in the vehicle and began to make-out for almost twenty minutes. The investigator in the car therefore entered the parking deck, picked up the other investigator and began to conduct stationary surveillance that eventually turned into following the car when they decided to leave the parking deck. The couple traveled to one of the highest-priced resorts in the area and settled in for the night.

During the next couple of days the investigators followed the pair through various mobile and foot surveillances as they took in all of the tourist sights. The documentation was obtained and the client was happy with the results.

Pedestrian to Bus surveillance

Special problem can be presented when a person leaves their house walking, enters a bus and then wonders around the downtown streets. It is fairly common for a subject to get on some form of public transportation such as a bus, subway, train or taxi. Surveillance of a subject in either a bus or taxi requires special attention because it is common for there to be several other taxis or buses in the vicinity that can easily cause confusion. It is therefore important to get the number of the bus or taxi for distinction purposes. Often times our agency has radioed another investigator who gets ahead of the bus, parks their vehicle and then gets on the bus with the subject. If that is not possible, mobile surveillance using more than one investigator greatly increases the effectiveness at this point.

Once the subject reaches their destination, the investigator has to be able to identify the subject as they get out of the public transportation. Sounds easy enough, but when you have 5-10 people getting off of a bus along with another 5-10 trying to get on, the subject can be lost. When the target is confirmed exiting the public transportation, the investigator has to quickly find a parking spot and pursue the subject on foot.

If the subject enters a building and gets on an elevator, you can handle this situation several ways. First, enter the elevator after the subject and let them push the floor button first and simply get off at the same floor. Depending on the amount of time you have been following the subject or if they appear to have a suspicious nature, this may not work. In addition, once the subject exits onto a particular floor, you still have to identify which office they go into. The investigator may want to get on the elevator with the subject, let them make the floor selection and then push the button for the floor right above theirs if the subject appears somewhat suspicious or nervous. The investigator can then come back down in another elevator or use the stairs to come back down. Chances are, you will not get back down in time to see which office the subject entered. However, surveillance can be conducted on the floor by simply "hanging out" in the hallway and waiting for the subject to come back out. If you believe the subject may be working in one of the offices the investigator may have to enter each office using a suitable pre-text to see which one they may have gone into. The obvious problem with this is that the subject may exit the building while the investigator is inside one of the offices.

If a subject enters a building and the investigator is relatively sure that they will only be in there for a short period of time and does not necessarily need to know where the subject went, an analysis still has to be made. The investigator should enter the lobby to see how many exits the building has, if there are stairs that exit into a parking deck or onto the street and similar items such as these. Some building have tunnels that link the building to other buildings and these conditions will determine whether or not you can remain outside and simply watch the front entrance or if you have to wait in the lobby.

An investigator should always attempt to fit into the

environment. While walking on foot, attention should be paid as to what the other people in the area are doing, what they are carrying and where they are going. If most of the people have some type of drink in their hands, pick up a cup and carry it around even if it is used. There may be vendors handing out circulars and other documents and the investigator should intentionally seek out these papers when walking by. Attention should be paid regarding where the majority of the people appear to be heading. If there is a party nearby, some type of group or association putting on a function or other obvious activity, the investigator should determine who they are and prepare themselves mentally in case they are approached. Following a subject is just part of the job. Fitting in, having an appropriate alibi and not making yourself "stand-out" is the difference between an investigator and a professional.

In addition, the investigator should always be thinking ahead and analyzing the area to determine possible concealment areas, dangerous situations such as being lead into a trap and places that the subject may be heading. While walking, take advantage of the reflective materials that will naturally be available. Use large plate glass windows commonly found on storefronts to observe the subject's reflection while appearing to be browsing and glancing into a store. Use the side view mirrors on cars to do the same and make it appear as though you are adjusting a contact or your hair. If you are a female investigator, use a make-up compact mirror to observe the subject. Male investigators can get away with carrying a small mirror in the palm of the hand for the same reason. However, care will have to be taken to make sure that the mirror does not reflect light and draw attention to the investigator. Other "covers" can be stopping to use your cell phone or to check or send a text message. If the subject stops abruptly, the investigator can bend down to tie a shoe, take a rock out of a shoe, pause and look lost or a host of other scenarios. The idea is to find something that you feel comfortable using and is something that your personality may do anyway to insure your actions are as natural as possible.

The idea that T.V. has portrayed the investigator changing identities, clothes, hats, etc… is great for T.V. but is not practical in real use (unless you practice). When you're following someone in a vehicle, these are not normally necessary. When you're following someone on foot, you can't carry the items with you and may have difficulty finding time to change unless you take time to practice these techniques in your off time. There are several tricks that can help, especially if you know ahead of time that the subject will travel on foot. At the very least, carry a baseball hat and another shirt with you. Whenever you get out of the vehicle, place the baseball hat in your back pocket and slip the shirt over the one you have on. As the surveillance goes on, you can remove the top shirt and put on the baseball hat to help change your appearance. In colder climates, this is even easier because you can use a coat and take the jacket on and off. It may be useful to purchase a coat that can turn inside out and be worn either way for even more variety. If the subject has been known to travel on foot, you may elect to put on several shirts and a pair of shorts under your pants. Taking one layer of clothing off may help the subject loose track of you. The investigator should also keep an average size gym bag, backpack or similar item readily available for these circumstances so that equipment can be carried in it and clothes can be placed inside as well.

Other ways of "hiding" when on foot surveillance include finding a couple or several people walking side-by-side. You can get close enough to not alarm them but close enough to use them as a shield (even temporarily). Walking as close to the buildings as possible also helps to take you out of a visual glance by the target. Keep an eye out for landscaping, large bushes, trees, trash receptacles, bicycle racks, newspaper stands or any similar device that you can use to hide behind temporarily. Of course you can't just suddenly squat down behind one of these without attracting attention. If you do squat down, rub your ankle, adjust your shoe or perform some related activity that would suggest to an onlooker that you had a reason for the behavior. In the right setting, you can always put on dark sunglasses, pick up a cup (or use your hat) and act like you are blind and seeking handouts.

The Hand Off

When you are fortunate enough to have the budget and manpower available, using the hand-off technique can be very useful. In this scenario, one investigator can walk on the parallel street and cut over in time to pick up the target crossing the street at an intersection. The initial investigator can enter a building, turn around (not preferred) or turn at the intersection and walk to the next parallel street and continue to mirror the target. Good communication is required between the investigators to successfully make this technique effective.

If there are two or more investigators, one may be able to locate a balcony, tall building or similar geographic location that will enable visual contact with the target. They can then communicate with the team without having to be directly near the target.

If you are in a location where there are rickshaws, horse-drawn wagons, rental bicycles or similar non-automotive carriages you may utilize this as your cover and continue the pursuit. You then have control over the speed in which the device is being peddled or steered.

As the investigator works more and more cases conducting foot surveillance, their confidence will become greater. Normally, investigators start out following subjects either too close or too far away. Through experience, the investigator will learn the right distance and when to move up or lay back some. Although foot surveillance can be difficult, it is usually not as trying as mobile surveillance. At least on foot surveillance you do not have to drive while following the subject. The art of foot surveillance is obviously one of the older methods of surveillance and will continue to be an evolving technique that will have to adjust with the times.

Reversing Direction

If the target suddenly reverses direction the PI should step into a store or keep on their current path. Any sudden deviation by the PI will most likely draw attention to the surveillance. It is very important to know your surroundings in the event the target attempts to check for a tail by walking into a dead-end street. If things appear to be getting tense and the target may be getting suspicious, *do not* turn a corner right after them. Instead cross the street and then make the corner:

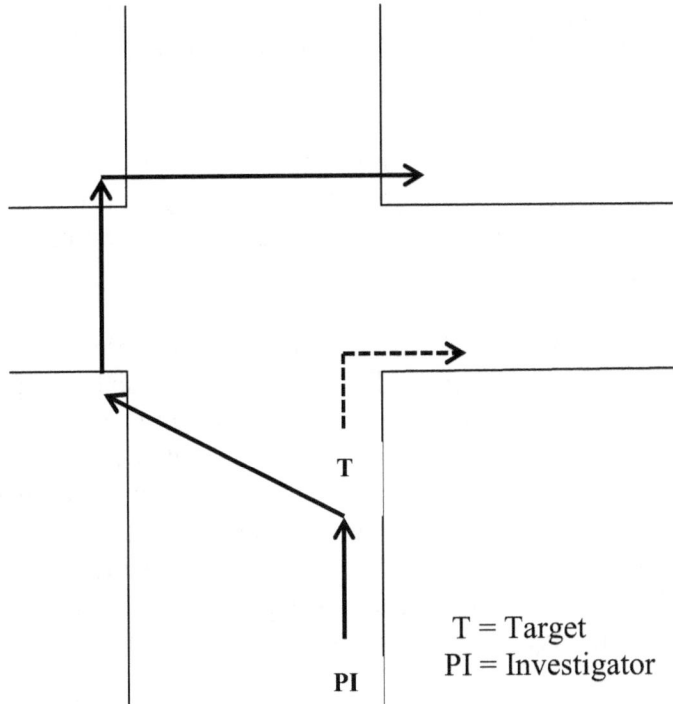

T = Target
PI = Investigator

There are numerous variations of this but the diagram gives you a general sense of the technique. Of course the investigator has to keep an eye on traffic to determine if and when you can make the crossings without delay.

In this day of technology it is certainly not unusual to be walking with your cell phone near your face while you are reading an email of texting. This also allows the opportunity to capture video with your cell phone. The best scenario is your being equipped with a covert camera for even better footage.

Be careful regarding picking up any discarded item the target may toss down. This could be a ploy to identify anyone who is tailing the target. If possible, you *may* be able to quickly photograph or video the item as you pass by but this would have to be very discrete.

A good investigator should always have cash with them in the event the person enters a theater, restaurant, taxi, subway or any other place where cash may be needed. A cover story should be developed that fits into the area such as your being a tourist out for a walk, you are on your way to meet your spouse, you brother just got a job in the area and you are trying to surprise him for lunch or a host of similar covers. The story might also change as you walk from one area to another. If the target starts by leaving an office building and walks into a nearby residential neighborhood the cover story would have to change accordingly.

Many of the same techniques used during mobile surveillance can apply to foot surveillance. The investigator has to be adaptive to their surroundings, maintain a good cover story and be ready for any possible confrontation. As in any surveillance, it is always better to let the person go than to get burned. The target may frequent the area and you can always set up surveillance the next day starting at the point where the surveillance was terminated the day before. Even if this is not the case, your investigation and cover remains in tack for another day.

MOBILE SURVEILLANCE AT IT'S BEST
Chapter Five

Mobile surveillance is one of the most exciting types of investigations because so much is happening at one time. The "cat and mouse game" is at it's best, pitting the investigator's skills and knowledge against plain old bad luck. Sometimes, regardless of the investigator's expertise, the subject is just going to be lost because of situations beyond your control. Having the light change to red and traffic stopping after your subject crossed through the intersection with no alternatives is probably the most common source of frustrations. Then there are the times when emergency vehicles, buses, trains, rude drivers and similar situations do not allow you to maintain sight of the subject. I can assure you that your stress level will rise whenever you have been sitting on a case for a long period of time and the first time the subject leaves, you loose them. You have to expect this because it's going to happen. You can even relate mobile surveillance to Murphy's Law that states, "If something can go wrong, something will go wrong". There are times when these things will happen and all you can do is get over it.

Although most investigators would like to work as a team with other investigators on a stakeout, this is usually not possible. In law enforcement agencies, team stakeouts are the norm. However, in the private sector money becomes the driving factor for using only one investigator. Any P.I. who has ever had to market their services knows that one of the first questions a potential client asks is, "how much do you charge per hour"? Often, this is a make or break situation and if you can't justify your hourly rate, everything you say after that will go in one ear and out the other.

Although our job as a P.I. is to discuss the case with the client and provide them with an analysis of how much time it will take to provide a successful investigation, the ultimate decision is the client's. There are always cycles in business, and the P.I. has to be aware of this. For instance, during the years of the oil bust and the savings and loan scandals, cases and the costs of these investigations were severely scrutinized. During fat years, the companies do not watch or dictate the expenses as closely. The P.I. has to adapt and be sensitive to these trends. Most insurance companies have one of several mind-sets involving the use of P.I.'s. For example, there are clients that will never authorize more than four hours of surveillance. With these clients, it is an act of Congress to get anymore hours authorized for surveillance. Then there are those clients that always ask for 24 hours of surveillance, broken down over three consecutive days. Most clients, however, fall in the middle. Clients, in general, are not willing to pay for more than one investigator on a case. The manager of a P.I. firm then has to make decisions based on safety, success and the monetary aspects of the investigation.

All investigators realize that an investigation's success is greatly enhanced by using more than one investigator. However, the manager of a P.I. agency has to balance the case load, making sure that each investigator's time is utilized in the best way possible, providing for as much of their time being billable hours as possible. To keep the profit margin where it should be on a case, the manager may be forced into using only one investigator. The use of more than one investigator boils down to how good a marketing person the P.I. is and how well they can convince their client to get off of their pocket book. Once this is decided, you can go on to formulating the strategy for conducting the actual surveillance.

Part of mobile surveillance is the preparation for surveillance. As you may recall, surveillance is the "art of discovering without being discovered". How you prepare and initiate the surveillance will have a direct effect on how long you will be able to conduct mobile surveillance without being detected. The first thing that an investigator has to do is be prepared. By this, I mean being mentally, physically and spiritually ready. The investigator cannot just pull up to a location and sit there. He must first prepare himself by checking the map to see the layout of streets and major intersections. Even though the investigator may know the area, the map should still be observed to check for hidden streets or changes that the investigator may not be aware of. The major streets and intersections should be noted because most people usually head towards the major streets since this is where restaurants, shopping areas and businesses are located. The investigator should also note the location of schools, whether or not the subject is known to have school age kids. If they do have young kids, you need to know where the subject may be going if they start in that direction. If they do not have school aged kids, you need to be aware of these areas so that you will pay more attention to traffic and pedestrians even if they go that way.

Although record searches have very little to do with the topic of surveillance, certain records should be researched before the investigator ever attempts to conduct surveillance. Without performing basic record searches, you may end up sitting for hours at a house where the subject doesn't actually live. Some of the basic and inexpensive searches should be directory assistance databases that are free. Search for a listing for the subject and get their *address and telephone number*. If the subject is a female, the listing may be in her husband's name that you may not know. Search for a listing for the subject and/or *any listing with the same last name on Main Street* (or whatever the name of the street is). The next record search should be through the county tax office. Most have their records on-line and are free to access. Search for any information on property owned by the subject. You may find that they own several pieces of property and the address you have may be a rental property. If there is only one listing, check for the property address *and* the mailing address as they may be different. It would not be a bad idea to see if there are any subjects with the same last name listed on the same street. That way you will know ahead of time and not wind up sitting in front of a relative's house.

If you do not have any luck with the tax office, check the county appraisal district office and research the same information. If there are still no listings by the subject's name, check for the owner of the property address you have been given for the subject. If you still do not have any information confirming the subject's address, check with the county's voter's registration office to see if they are a listed voter. If so, their address will be listed and in some situations you can also get their social security number, date of birth, place of birth and similar information. Depending on the nature of the investigation, you may want to check with the county's assumed name records to see if the subject owns a business. Often times, people run businesses out of their homes and the banks usually require at least an assumed name certificate before the party can open a commercial bank account. If this information provides a listing or if you want to check further on a business, conduct on-line research at the State Comptroller (sometimes called the State Treasurer, State Tax Office, etc.) as they are responsible for collecting taxes on businesses. The office will be able to tell you who the owners are, their addresses, if they are incorporated and similar information. The Secretary of State's office is also another office to check with because corporations have to file their corporate papers with this office and you can learn the owner's, addresses, parent company and related information.

Almost all of the searches mentioned above can be done by telephone and/or free Internet access. However, they will save you time and the client money if you do your homework before you ever start. The next item of preparation is equipment. This includes your vehicle. There is no need in setting up surveillance if the vehicle does not have sufficient gas, does not have clean windows to see out of and is not safe and ready for use. Following someone around with a limited amount of gas may cause you to have to drop the surveillance to go get gasoline. Having windows that are not clean will cause your eyes to strain and the video to blur and should never occur. Take a few minutes to take care of these items and they will prove to be a benefit.

After taking care of the mental preparation, the investigator should consider the spiritual preparation. Although I do not consider myself a "preacher", I have found that I am more effective when I take the time to pray for guidance on a case, for protection and for success. I can tell you that I can tell a dramatic difference in those cases where I have taken the time to pray versus failing to pray. There are times when you may loose a person and ask for spiritual guidance to relocate the subject. I can tell you that it works and is not merely coincidence.

Preparing your equipment and vehicle for surveillance is an important issue that can't be overlooked. Failing to maintain the equipment and not being ready will come back to haunt you if you're not careful.

On the subject of vehicles, you need to realize that all vehicles are not suited for surveillance. Take for instance, vans. Although they provide the greatest comfort for the investigator, the average person who thinks of investigators doing surveillance almost always think of them in a van. That's one strike against you. In addition, full-size vans normally attract too much attention, are more difficult to drive, need more space to park and take more gas. The best vehicles are the ones that you see the most of because they can mix into most areas the best. I personally prefer the smaller SUV and or cross-overs because they are common enough, provide sufficient room inside, are O.K. on gas and sit higher off the ground. Being higher than a lot of cars will provide better viewing in traffic and parking lots and the whole vehicle sits higher, which will prevent damage to the vehicle in rough terrain or when you have to cross over concrete medians and things of that nature. Depending on the size of the company and the number of investigators, you may need a variety of vehicles. The vehicles that are used have to be able to blend into all types of socio-economic areas. The vehicle has to be acceptable in poverty stricken areas as well as the average and upper class subdivisions.

The vehicle that you choose should also be nice, but average. The vehicle should not be one that turns heads when you drive by someone. Unlike the show Magnum, P.I., driving a luxury car around like the actor did would cause attention to be drawn to you and make you ineffective. The investigator should also remember that even things like bumper stickers, special hub-caps, special lights and things of this nature may be just the item that catches a person's attention.

On the subject of lights, proper lighting can be a useful tool. Exterior fog lights can help to change the look of the vehicle at night. When following a subject at night, follow the subject for a while with just the regular lights on. After following the subject for a while and at the proper time (not when you and they are the only ones on the road), turn the fog lights on to change the appearance of your vehicle. I have even known investigators who have vehicles with fog lights mounted on the vehicle at the factory, but who put an additional set of lights inside the grill to give them a third look.

Another useful item that may require you to hunt up a friend who is a mechanic is what is known as a "kill switch". This is a wire that is connected to the solenoid and when you throw the switch inside (or one mounted on the exterior), the engine sounds like it wants to start, but the kill switch does not allow it to. This may give you the opportunity to get in some places that you need an excuse for being there. For example, if you have a subject in a rural area and they are out chopping wood or something else that you need to blow your cover to get, you may have to use this. The investigator, assuming that there is no other way or location to get the video, may have to drive down the road, cut the engine off and coast to a good surveillance position. Throw the kill switch and attempt to start the car several times, and of course it won't start. You can then get out and raise the hood and look at the engine. If need be, you can get your cellular telephone out and walk around making it look as if you are calling help or are calling your mechanic to ask him what to do. Once you have set the stage, you can then get back into the vehicle and shoot video while you "are waiting" on help. Once you get the video you need, you can hit the kill switch and start the engine again. If anyone asks, you can simply tell them that the engine sometime quits when it gets hot and you haven't had time (or haven't had the money) to get it fixed.

Once the type of vehicle and the maintenance of the vehicle have been properly addressed, you now have to prepare the *inside* for use. I would suggest purchasing a cigarette lighter adapter that has three outlets. This will allow you to power your video camera, cellular telephone and a laptop computer from the engine's battery. Attempting to use the video camera with only the battery that comes with the camera is *not going to work* over a long period of time. There is nothing worse than having your subject working on the engine of a car and the camera battery running out of power! Some investigators may elect to purchase a small TV and hand held video games and power them from the cigarette lighter. I would caution you against the T.V. and video games, as well as reading books and similar things as they may distract you and your subject may drive away while your watching T.V.

Once the inside power issue is taken care of, the next item is concealment. The investigator should have already had the vehicle windows tinted as dark as the State laws allow. Incidentally, some States prohibit any type of window tint and you may need to check before doing this. Assuming that your state allows window tinting, you now need to make the interior so dark that if someone (possibly your subject) came up to the vehicle and tried to look inside, they would not be able to do so. Not only will this prevent you from getting caught, but it will also provide a sense of security and confidence. The main area to concentrate on is the driver's area, possibly the back passenger area of the vehicle if you are the type of investigator who is prone to climbing in the back to conduct surveillance. Whatever area you commonly use, prepare it properly by preventing as much sunlight from coming in as possible. Sunlight that comes in the passenger compartment will tend to be like a spotlight on you and every move you make will be seen (including holding up a video camera).

First, start with the largest area that lets sunlight in; the front windshield. In States that allow window tinting, you can usually have a 1-2 inch section of tint placed from about the rear-view mirror up to the edge of the roof. Secondly, invest in 2-3 cardboard window visors, making sure that each has a different design and that each design is as plain as possible to prevent unnecessary attention from being drawn to your vehicle. I suggest buying 2-3 different kinds because as you follow a person around town all day, you should switch the visor from time-to-time to present a different image. I would tend to stay away from the silver reflective type of visors and the kind that open up like shades because they are not as prominent and are more noticeable. When your sitting still, these visors will help keep you cooler and make people think that your vehicle is an empty, parked car.

Next, you should invest in a small curtain rod and some dark material for curtains. Most curtain rods are expandable and will fit the different vehicles easily. You can come up with some elaborate mechanism to hold the curtain rods, or you can simply pinch the ends flat and bend them so that you can stick the ends in the interior trim panels that run around the top of the car's roof. If there is not trim panels to stick this in, there is usually trim (hard plastic) panels that run up and down between the front doors and the back door inside the vehicle and the ends can be put in the top of these. You can then make some curtains that will slide on the curtain rod, and preferably be in two separate pieces. Having the curtains in two separate pieces will allow you to pull them back out of your way easier, you can use the slit in the middle to open slightly when backing up or you can use the slit between the curtains to shoot video through. When your conducting surveillance, keep the curtains down to block out the sunlight. When your finished for the day, you can pull them open and use Velcro to hold them in place, tie them back or pull them up and hold them up against the roof using the hand grips that some vehicles have on the roof above the back doors.

Next are the front passenger and driver's door windows. Most States that allow window tinting require that the tint on these two windows be a little lighter than the rest. You should also remember when you are getting the tint that your vehicle will have to pass State inspections and getting them darker than what is legal will cause you to have to strip the tint off to pass the inspection. The tint on these two windows is typically not dark enough to prevent someone from seeing you inside the vehicle. To make up for this, you can cut plexi-glass in the same shape as the windows, leaving them slightly shorter to allow you to easily put them in and out. Once the plexi-glass is cut, you can put additional window tint on these that will make the windows too dark to see in.

For those States that prohibit window tinting, you may have to go to plan "B". You can purchase window shades that have suction cups on them and allow you to stick these on the glass. They also have small holes in them which video can be shot through without obstructing the video. You can pull these down and obstruct a person's view. They may be able to tell that there is someone in the vehicle, but can't see that you are holding up a video camera. However, the investigator may still be able to use the window tint and Plexiglas idea while parked, and can remove them while driving to prevent being stopped for illegal window tint.

Once these items have been taken care of, you need to learn how to use these properly. Pulling up on a street at 3:00 in the afternoon and throwing up the window visor and curtains with people and kids standing around watching is not effective and will get the police called on you. The only time you should do this is when you have no other choice and can do this for just long enough to get the video you need. Most of the time, you can put these items up when you arrive at a case early in the morning before everyone starts leaving for work. When you follow someone to a mall or place of business, you can easily put these items to work without causing any suspicions.

There are numerous techniques that can be used when concealment is not possible but giving the appearance of a parked and unoccupied vehicle is the best. When this is not possible, the investigator can sit in the passenger seat to give the appearance that they are waiting on someone. The investigator can also raise the headrests on the seats to help obstruct the view of their body from behind. In addition, the investigator may wish to hang clothes in the back seat to block the view of persons passing by.

After the vehicle is properly prepared, you have to turn your attention to the equipment itself. This includes having extra memory cards on hand. I am usually pretty good about this, however, one time I had switched vehicles with another investigator and was in a different city. I had followed this guy all day and had gotten some pretty good video of him. He was changing the tire on a car when the indicator on the video camera started flashing to let me know I was nearing the end of the storage capacity. Fortunately, he was finishing his task and he went inside the house. I took the chance and drove about a half a mile to a grocery store and ran in and purchased a couple of more memory card since I couldn't find an extra one in the vehicle. I got back to the guy's house just in time to see him leave and go to a friend's house where they got involved working on another car. This could have been a disastrous situation and one that was uncalled for.

Another item of concern is condensation. If a camera is left in a car over-night and the temperature is very cold, or very hot, when you get into the vehicle and turn on the heat or air conditioner, the camera may have condensation. If this occurs, the camera will not function and could cause some problems for a short period of time until it dries out. It is a good idea to take the camera in and out of the vehicle at night to prevent this, as well as for security reasons.

It is a good idea to prepare your vehicle with extra items that you may not need all of the time such as cover-alls. If you ever need to hit the weeds to conduct surveillance, you need a pair of earth colored cover-alls for concealment and to protect your clothes. Throwing in extra clothes, hats, boots, bags and things of this type will also help out. Unlike some of the T.V. shows, costumes and disguises are not an everyday part of surveillance and is seldom ever needed.

Other things that you may want to consider include a container of drinking water, snacks, an ice chest and a towel. If you are forced to sit in a hot vehicle, your body may need some water to prevent dehydration. You may also need a towel to wipe off sweet. I like to carry a dark colored towel to throw over my video camera for concealment as well. Another source of concern is caffeine. Although all the T.V. shows show the investigators sitting around drinking coffee, you should consider how that effects your body. You may find that you need to cut back on drinks that contain caffeine because it requires you to use the bathroom too frequently. It never fails, you can be sitting on a house for four hours and when you decide to run around the corner to use the bathroom, the subject leaves. Sometimes, the investigator will get in situations where they can't leave, but still have to use the bathroom. You may want to find some type of container that will allow you to relieve yourself in these situations.

Finally, all of the preparations have been done and you're ready to start surveillance! The needs of your clients and the goals of the investigation will determine how and when the surveillance will be conducted. If the case involves a worker's compensation, injury related case or something similar, you will have to start surveillance early to see if they are going to work. You will also have to cover the hours around 3:00 P.M. to see if they leave for a 3:00-11:00 P.M. shift. If you suspect that they may be working a night job, surveillance will have to be initiated at the proper times to determine this. Surveillance on a domestic case will depend on the times that the client suspects that the partner may be engaging in their activities. All other cases are subject to the needs of the clients.

Setting the initial groundwork for the surveillance is important. For instance, if the location in which you will conduct surveillance is in a small suburb or a rural area, you may want to call the police dispatcher and let them know who you are, the street you will be on and the type of vehicle that you will be in so that it will prevent marked units from converging on you after neighbors call. Once you arrive at the general location, you need to positively identify the house. The subject's house and the neighbors may not have house numbers displayed. If this is the case, you will have to figure out how the other houses on the street are spaced out. For example, you may find that a house has the number 2128, the next one is 2132 and the next is 2136. You now know that the houses are numbered in increments of "4" and should be able to count the houses until you figure out which one is the subject's. Once this is done, check the registrations on the vehicles parked at the house to make sure they match the house number and the subject. This sounds basic, but you will be surprised at how easy it is to assume that you have the right house and not double-check it.

Once you have identified the house, try to find a landmark that will assist you in identifying the house from a distance. If a car backs out of a garage, you can use these things to keep you from chasing the wrong subject. Some of the items to use are light poles, unusual mailboxes, trees, fences, trashcans and things of this nature. After identifying the house and landmarks, you now need to validate the information in your case preparation. Check the subdivision out, the adjoining streets and routes so that you will not be surprised when you find out there is a back exit to the subdivision that the subject went out and that you didn't even know existed. You are now ready to "set-up" surveillance. For more information on this, review the Chapter on Stationary Surveillance.

There are several basic concepts and factors to keep in mind when following a subject. One factor is whether or not the subject's vehicle has a rear-view mirror, side mirrors, both or neither. Most vehicles have mirrors but check to see if they are adjusted properly or is it pointing down at the seat or at the driver? The driving characteristics of the subject will play a part in how you follow the subject. Pay attention to the driver to see how often they check their mirrors. Some drivers constantly check while others seldom look. This could have a barring on how close you can follow the subject. Another characteristic to check is whether or not the subject uses their turn signals. If they do, how much distance do they leave between the turn signal indication and the place they turn? The speed that the subject drives is another factor. Some drivers characteristically drive extremely fast everywhere they go, some drive the speed limit, while others drive unusually slow. You will have to adjust accordingly.

Let's say that the subject you are following pulls out of their driveway and heads down the street. You immediately take off, right? Wrong. Usually, as soon as a person pulls onto a street they check their mirrors. Give the subject several seconds to check the mirror so that your vehicle moving will not catch their eye while they are checking the mirror. Initially, following the subject onto several different streets will not be a problem. However, if they keep turning on different residential streets it may get obvious if the subject and the investigator's vehicles are the only ones on the road.

There are several techniques that are useful to help defuse any suspicions on the part of the target, especially in residential areas. One is the timing between the subject's vehicle and the investigator's vehicle when the subject makes a turn. Take every opportunity to coast, putting your vehicle in neutral momentarily if needed. Try to do this without pushing on the break and making the tail-lights activate, especially at night. You should attempt to time it so that just as the subject turns, the investigator arrives at the intersection in perfect time sequence to see the back of the car (see diagram).

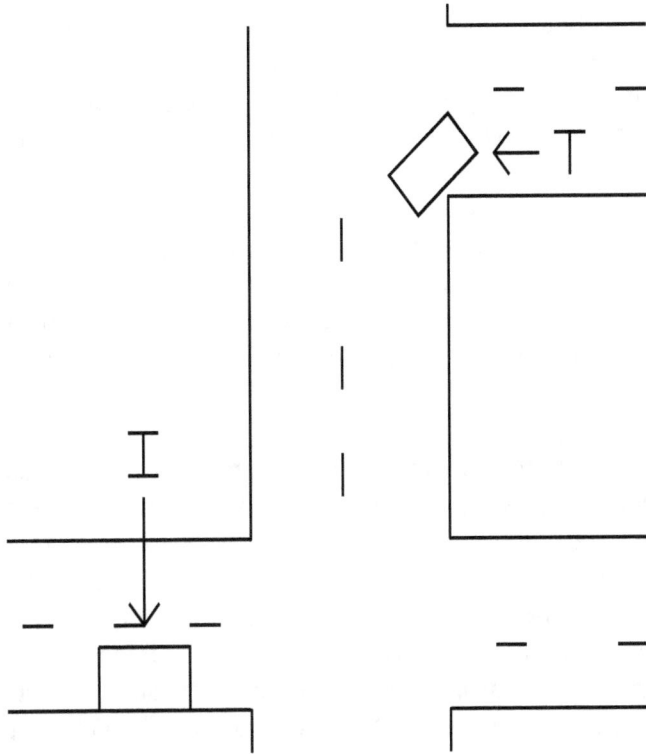

I = Investigator
T = Target Subject

In the diagram, the investigator is approaching the intersection after the target has turned left. As the investigator does so, they get to the intersection just in time to see the target vehicle make another turn to the right. The position of the target vehicle does not allow the driver to use their mirrors to check the vehicles behind them. The problem with this technique is that the timing has to be just right or you may not know which way the subject turned.

Another technique is pulling over on the side of the road periodically and using parked cars to shelter your vehicle. If a subject is traveling down residential streets, continuing to come up directly behind them at stop signs and intersections will cause suspicions. To avoid this, you can pull over against the curb. When doing this, you have to appear to have a legitimate reason for doing so. This is especially effective at intersections with traffic lights. If the subject is approaching a traffic light that is just turning red, it may be advisable to pull over behind a parked car and wait until the light changes before continuing. Caution should be used that you do not allow too many vehicles to go by and get between you and the subject or you may get caught behind traffic and not make the light yourself. You should also look for advantages such as houses with circular driveways without any vehicles in the drive. Instead of pulling against the curb, you can turn into the driveway, pause momentarily and then pull back onto the road. You now have alleviated suspicions because you could have been dropping someone off, checking the mail for a friend or any number of similar excuses.

When you turn the corner onto a new residential street behind the subject, try to stay to the right next to the curb and use obstructions like parked cars as long as possible to block the subject's view of your vehicle. Continuing to think of these types of things are absolutely necessary for the success of the surveillance. Occasionally, however, you will loose the subject or get the instinct that you should drop the surveillance because of suspicions. When this occurs, you may want to pick up the subject at approximately the same spot and at the same time in a day or two, remembering that people are creatures of habit and they probably take the same route most of the time. An example of the "curb" technique is outlined in the following diagram.

As you can see, by turning right and staying as close to the curb as possible, the target vehicle may not know where the investigator is at because of using the natural obstructions of the parked cars. Even if the target was able to see the investigator's vehicle, they still will not know if you let someone out or had other short-term business at that location.

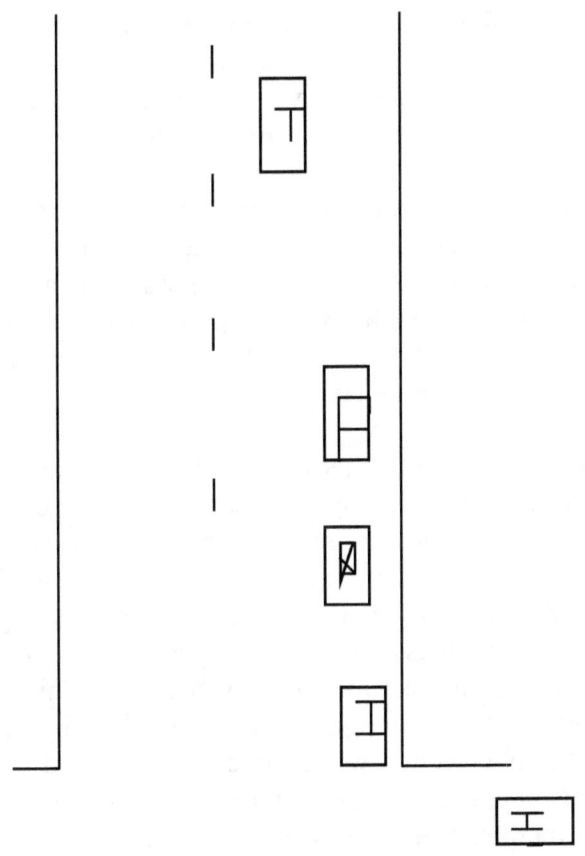

"THE CURB TECHNIQUE"

I = Investigator
T = Target/Subject
P = Parked Cars

Once the subject is out of a residential area and on a well-traveled road with other vehicles, mixing into the crowd becomes easier. While other vehicles provide new opportunities for concealment, the other vehicles become an obstacle course that the investigator will have to maneuver around in order to keep up with the target. You now have those who are driving too slow in the right hand lane, a slow moving vehicle in the left lane or similar problems. You will have to learn how to watch the subject's car through the windows of vehicles in between yours and the subject. Or you may have to watch the subject's tires under the large truck in front of you. Other techniques include moving over to the left in your lane as close to the white strip as possible to allow you to look down the sides of the other vehicles to keep an eye on the subject's car. This also works on the right side and the shoulder of the road can be an asset in this situation.

On main roads with other traffic, you will eventually get caught at a red light just as the subject's vehicle gets through the intersection. There are numerous techniques that can be applied in this situation. One is to simply check the intersection for other traffic and police officers and then run the red light. This is dangerous for obvious reasons and may cause an accident or get you a traffic ticket. In addition, if the subject is suspicious, they will know that you ran the light because you are the only vehicle moving through the intersection while the cars beside and behind you are remaining stopped. I cannot condone this action, however, it is an effective method of dealing with this situation.

The next way of dealing with red lights when the subject made it through the light would be to wait on the light to turn green and then speed up to close the distance between the two vehicles. This will have to be done just right or you will end up getting caught at another traffic light just ahead. Most traffic signals are set to prevent traffic from having the opportunity to build up much speed before they have to stop at another light. Keep this in mind because if you get caught in the sequence of red lights while the subject is able to get all greens, you never will catch them. When this occurs, you will have to speed up and try to get in the same sequence of lights as the subject.

Then there are the cases when the subject is in the right lane and you are 4-5 vehicles behind when the subject makes a right hand turn on a red. If you know the area and are sure that there is nowhere else for the subject to turn off within a short distance, you can wait patiently and then catch up. However, if you are uncertain, the investigator should attempt to cut-through a business or parking lot to continue on. This brings up the next point, which is to keep enough distance between your vehicle and the one in front of you so that you do not get trapped and are unable to maneuver. You should also pay attention to the traffic coming from the left of you if you are trying this because there may be so much traffic that you will end up getting caught in the parking lot and could have made it out faster by waiting back at the light. You also should glance at the parking lot that you are entering because some businesses put up obstacles to prevent people from cutting through their property and you may find that the only way out is back through the entrance driveway you just entered. An example of this technique is shown in the following diagram:

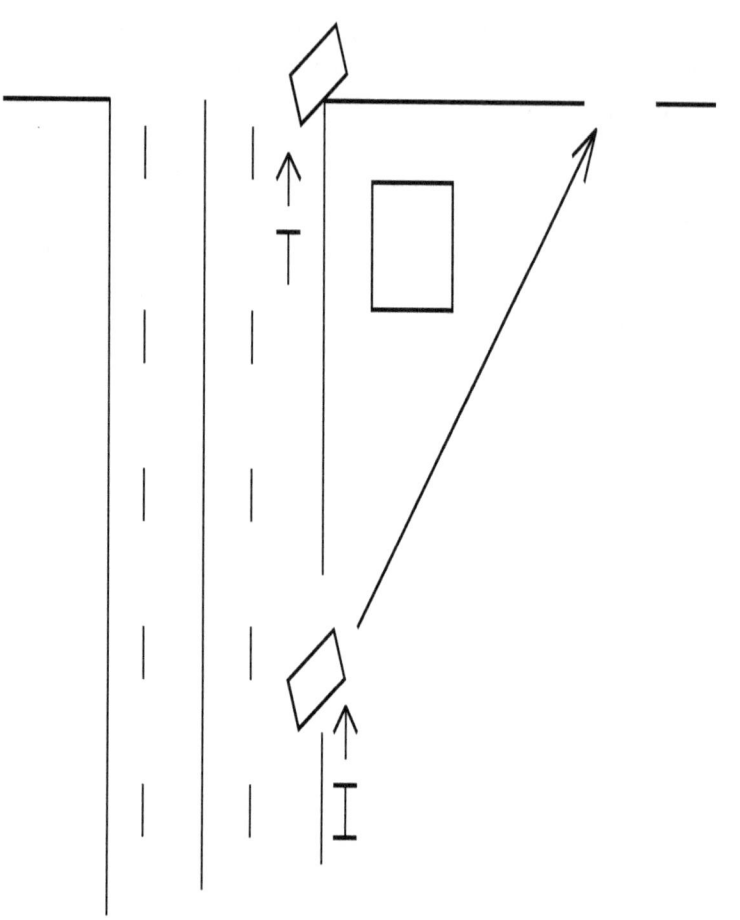

I = Investigator
T = Target/Subject

As you can see from this diagram, the building on the corner will help prevent the subject from seeing you turn into the parking lot. Hopefully, vehicles in the parking lot will also hide your vehicle while you make your way through the lot.

Then there is another way of dealing with red lights if the subject is going straight through the intersection and you got caught at the light. This technique has been given the nickname of the " U-turn return". An example of this is as follows:

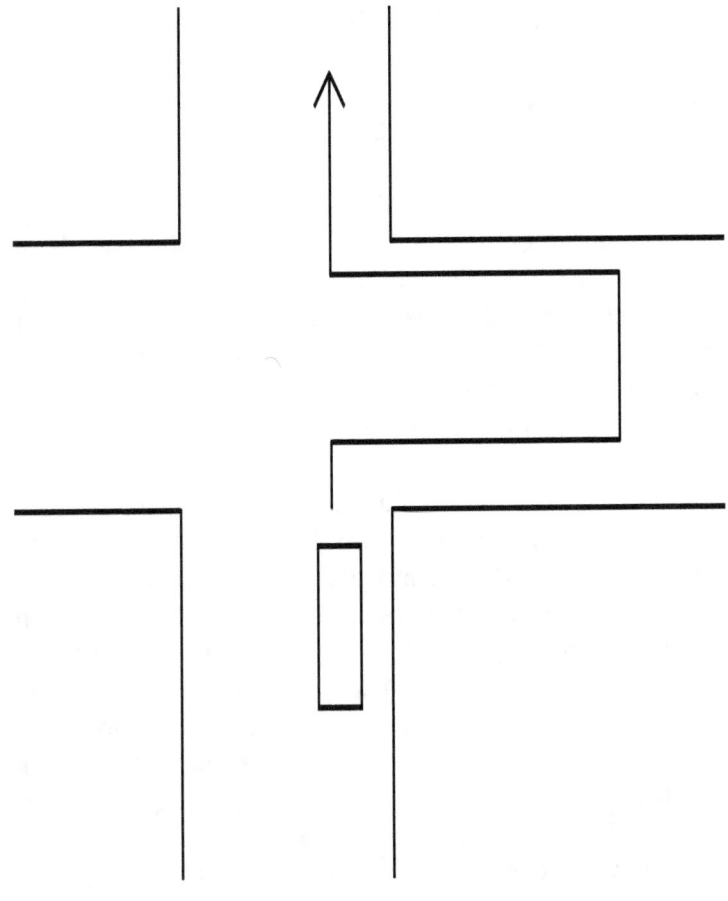

THE "U-TURN RETURN"

If you are the first vehicle caught at the light, you can stop for the red light, make a right hand turn on red, go a short distance, make a left hand turn or "U-turn" and head back the opposite way to the same intersection. Once back at the light, you can either turn on a green light or if it is turning red, make another right turn on a red light where you will now be behind the subject once again. Unless there is a "no U-turn sign posted", you have been able to run the intersection without officially running a red light.

As you can see, this can be a very useful technique that does not require a tremendous amount of effort. The investigator needs to be particularly careful when making the U-turn, however, to prevent any accidents from occurring.

Sometimes, if you are the only other vehicle that is pulling up to a traffic light and do not want to be behind or beside the subject, a convenience store/gas station is a useful cover. If one happens to be on the corner, pull up to a gas pump as if you are checking out the price of the gas or getting gas. After the light turns green, and hopefully a few cars have caught up, simply pull back out onto the road and keep following the subject.

Another effective technique on roads that have a lane in the middle designated as a turn lane is used when the subject is approaching a red light and you don't want to be near them. Pull into the turn lane and wait (assuming there is traffic coming which would normally prohibit a driver from making a turn). Once the light turns, you can pull back out into the traffic and continue. This is also a good place to station yourself if the subject appears to be somewhat lost and is unsure which parking lot or business they are looking for.

We have seen how to handle residential streets, main streets and intersections, but what about highways? These can be the easiest or the hardest types of mobile surveillance. During rush hour traffic, cars are switching lanes back and forth, cars are merging onto the highway and there are similar looking cars on the road. Throw in the sun in your eyes and you have the makings for a tough time. Just as difficult are the times when almost no one is on the highways except you and the subject. This provides for very little cover and doesn't really get weird until the subject exits the highway and you continue to follow them. For the most part, however, following the subject on the highway allows you to back off a little more than usual and the other vehicles provide good concealment.

There are some basic concepts that the investigator needs to learn and keep in mind when following someone on the highway. First, people tend to check their mirrors more on the highway. Fortunately, most people only pay attention to the vehicle directly behind or beside them. If the investigator keeps at *least* 4-5 behind the subject and stays in a different lane, the subject will probably never notice that they are being followed. When traffic allows, the investigator should attempt to keep even more vehicles between them when the traffic is moving steadily. There are times to close the gap between the subject and the investigator, such as when an intersection with another highway is coming up. You need to make sure that you see the subject's vehicle clearly and are at a proper distance to react without being noticed. As an example, if the subject is in the far left lane and you are in the same lane and 4-5 vehicles back, you may be setting yourself up to loose the subject. If the target vehicle abruptly crosses 2-3 lanes of traffic to get to an exit that they didn't see, you may be unable to cross the lanes and follow due to traffic congestion. In addition, when a subject crosses several lanes of traffic and takes an exit, an investigator making the same abrupt move will definitely draw attention to themselves.

This situation is another reason why the investigator always attempts to stay at least one lane over from the target. If the exits are all to the right side of the highway, attempt to stay one lane further to the right than the subject. The subject may start in the fast lane and you should therefore be in the next lane to the right. When the subject moves into your lane, the investigator should attempt to move over to the right one more lane *before* the subject has time to do so. If the investigator changes lanes first, it appears that the subject is mimicking the investigator instead of the other way around. There are some highways that have exits or lanes that merge onto other highways that veer off to the left. If the target is approaching one of these, the investigator should prepare for this and move into the left lane behind the subject or at least drive in a position where there are no vehicles to the left and a change of lane can easily be made. When people change lanes 2-3 at a time, this can usually mean one of several things. First, the subject may not know where they are going and saw their exit at the last minute. Secondly, they may be on to the investigator and that is their way of loosing the tail. Or, the person may just be a terrible driver and that is the way they drive everywhere! A good example of how you should position your vehicle while following someone on an expressway is as follows:

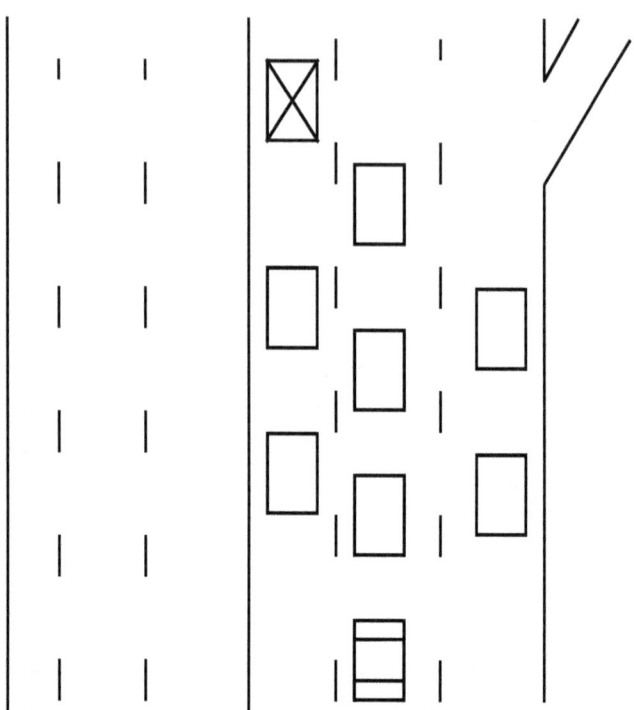

SURVEILLANCE ON AN EXPRESSWAY
(Preceding Diagram)

Target = Vehicle with an "X"
Investigator = Vehicle with two lines

From this diagram, you can see how a typical surveillance situation on an expressway should look. The investigator may have to move closer to the strip on their left to see down the side of the other cars. Even when the traffic seems to be moving properly, it is still important to keep the proper distance between the cars so that if the cars start stopping, you can still maneuver out of your lane and into another to continue pursuit.

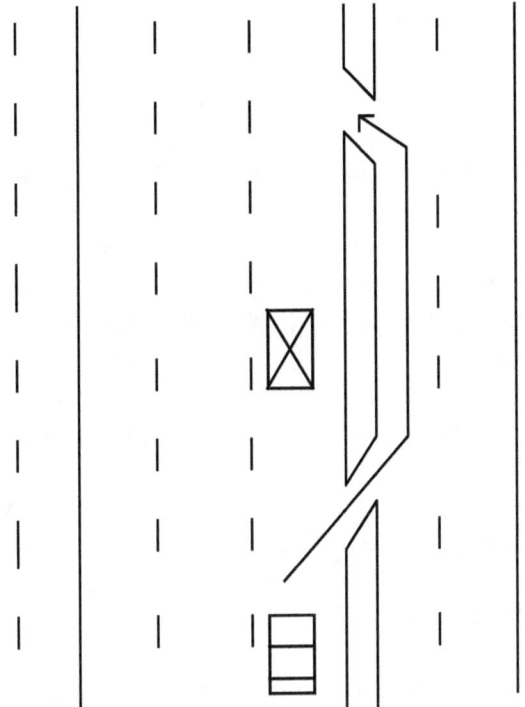

USING THE ACCESS ROAD DURING SURVEILLANCE

Investigator = Vehicle with two lines
Target = Vehicle with X

If an investigator knows the area well, they may choose to exit the highway and travel a short distance on the access road before returning onto the highway. This should typically not be tried if there is a traffic light at the end of the exit ramp before you can continue on as you may get held up too long. An example of this technique is in the preceding diagram.

The idea of this type of technique is to allow the target subject to continue on the highway while letting your vehicle get out of sight for a short distance. Of course, while on the access road, you should be able to continue to visually judge where the subject is in reference to yourself and you can slow down if necessary to allow you to come back on the highway *behind* the subject once again. This is particularly good to use if you are following a subject who drives slowly or below the speed of the other traffic.

Of course, there are those times when you accidentally get ahead of the subject on the highway because traffic in the subject's lane stops and your lane doesn't. You obviously cannot follow someone if you're ahead of them. If this occurs, attempt to move into the lane where the traffic is stopped and position your vehicle with the side-view mirrors where you can look back at the subject. If, like most people, the subject gets the opportunity to pull into another lane and continue, they probably will. However, they may be content in staying where they are. You should then attempt to move to the far right lane (slow lane) and intentionally slow down until the subject catches up.

Another common technique often used when following a vehicle is to place your vehicle into "neutral" to naturally slow down your vehicle without having to step on the brake. This is particularly useful when following someone at night because the subject may notice that you tend to slow down at the same time they do for no apparent reason. If you vehicle is a manual shift, you can easily downshift into a lower gear to create the same effect. This can also be utilized when the subject takes an exit ramp off of the highway and you are the only vehicle behind them. It may be possible to slow the vehicle down while you are still on the expressway and allow more space to get between you and the suspect vehicle.

Up to this point, we have discussed mobile surveillance geared primarily towards the use of a single investigator. If the case warrants the use of additional investigators, and assuming you have more investigators available, the surveillance should only get easier. A lot of the same techniques are used, however, with more vehicles following the subject, the subject is less likely to notice anyone following them. An example is in the following diagram:

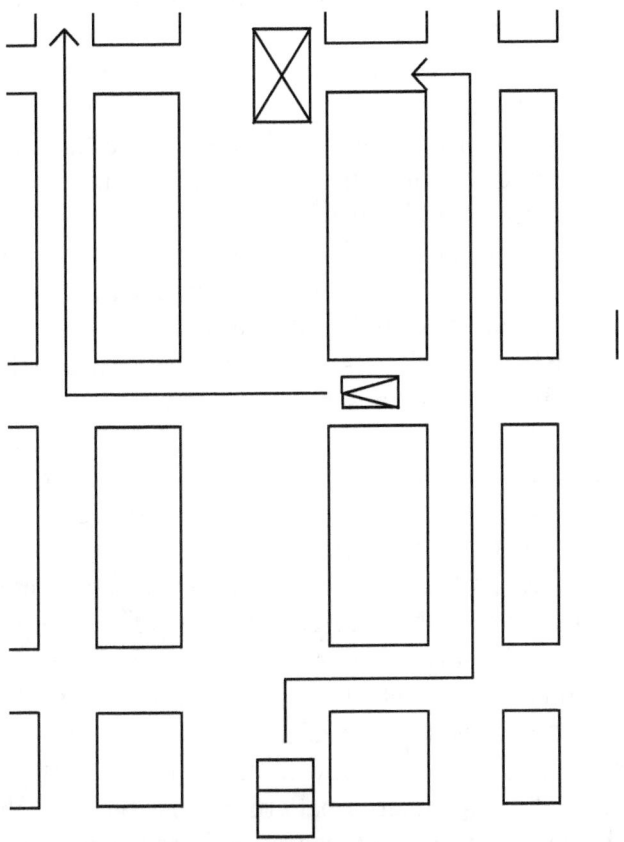

THE " CRISS-CROSS PATTERN "

Investigator # 1 = Vehicle with two lines
Investigator # 2 = Vehicle with <
Target Subject = Vehicle with X

In a residential area, the use of another investigator helps to curtail any noticeable surveillance from the very beginning. Once the subject pulls out of their house, the investigator who has direct observation of the house should radio to another investigator on the next street or at the edge of the subdivision. The second investigator can then pick-up the subject away from the home, allowing the first investigator to sit still until the subject has completely left their street. The first investigator can then communicate with the other investigator and catch up to both a little further down the road.

Following a subject who uses residential streets becomes quite a bit easier when there are other investigators involved. When this occurs, you can use techniques such as the "criss-cross pattern" or the "parallel technique" (see preceding diagram). The criss-cross pattern allows one investigator to always "have eyes" on the subject, although no investigator is directly behind the subject. This occurs through a combination of leapfrog moves and criss-cross patterns. One investigator can turn-off to the right or left and then proceeds to the next street. They then turn and become parallel to the subject and eventually pass the subject. Once they get ahead of the target, they can turn back and "criss-cross" the street in which the subject is on. After the subject goes by the intersection, the investigator moves up to the intersection and sits until the next investigator can conduct the same pattern. An example of this technique is outlined in the preceding diagram. The investigator designated with the < mark gets ahead of the subject and waits for the target to go by. The investigator can sit back away from the intersection and then after the subject goes by, move closer to watch the back of the subject's vehicle. The other investigator (designated by the two lines) waits to initiate this pattern until the other investigator is ahead and in position. The investigator then turns off and quickly moves to a position ahead of the target and waits for the subject to pass. The two investigators now start a pattern of criss-crossing the subject's path. This leapfrog can take place as long as the subject remains on a straightforward path. Once the subject turns left or right, this can be reinstituted and the criss-cross pattern adjusted to make up for the change in direction.

This pattern gets even easier if you have three or four investigators. In that case, you can continue to have one of four vehicles behind the subject at all times and as the next investigator is approached, they turn in behind the subject and the investigator that is behind the subject turns off and takes the place of the investigator who turned behind the subject. The pattern should be expanded to cover more ground before an investigator turns in behind the subject and takes the place of another investigator. You should be able to travel a minimum of ten blocks at a time before a change is made in the investigators. If you change too often, this may become strange to the subject in itself.

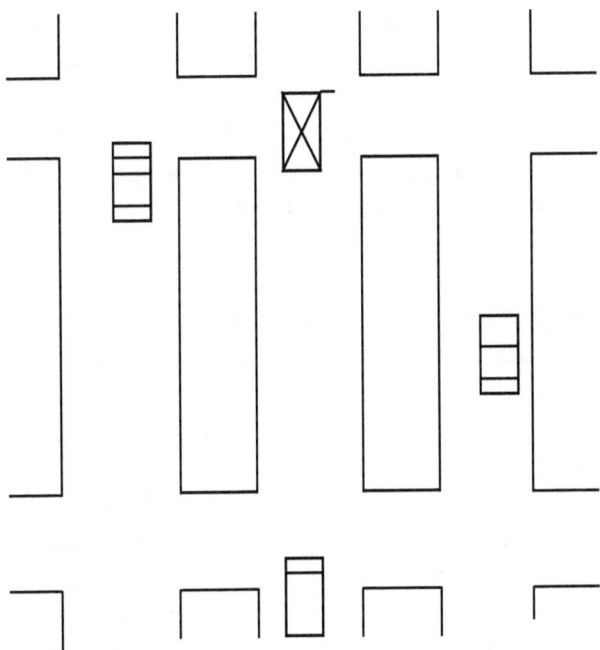

THREE INVESTIGATOR PARALLEL TECHNIQUE

Investigator # 1 = Vehicle with one line
Investigator # 2 = Vehicle with two lines
Investigator # 3 = Vehicle with three lines
Subject/Target = Vehicle with X

    In the preceding diagram, you will see how the parallel technique can be used. Once again, you can do this several different ways depending on the suspicious nature of the subject and the number of investigators used. If there are three or more investigators, you can have one traveling on the same street behind the subject while the other investigators continue on parallel streets with the subject. One investigator should be 1-2 streets over to the left of the subject while the other runs a parallel street 1-2 streets over to the right of the subject. After a sufficient amount of territory has been covered, one of the units traveling parallel can turn and take the place of the investigator following the subject, allowing the investigator to turn off, get out of sight for awhile and take over the position of the previous investigator. After this set-up has gone on for awhile, the third investigator can then move in behind the subject and take the place of the previous investigator with the leap-frog continuing.

In this situation, investigator # 3 should move up and pause at the intersection to visually observe the subject while the first investigator turns off and investigator # 2 turns in behind the subject.

Following subjects on main streets with several other investigators make the job much easier because one investigator can stay at the traffic light visually watching the subject while the other investigators attempt to by-pass the red light by cutting through parking lots and using other similar techniques. You can also be more risky and can pull up next to the subject vehicle to get a better look at the occupants. In addition, having 2-3 more cars around, even though they are investigators, may help alleviate any suspicions. If the person turns into a parking lot, having other investigators permits one investigator to turn in a driveway before the one the subject turned into. Another investigator can pass the drive-way the subject turned into while a third vehicle can either enter the lot with the subject or turn off and enter a parking lot across from the one the subject's vehicle turned into. For a visual description of this, refer to the following diagram:

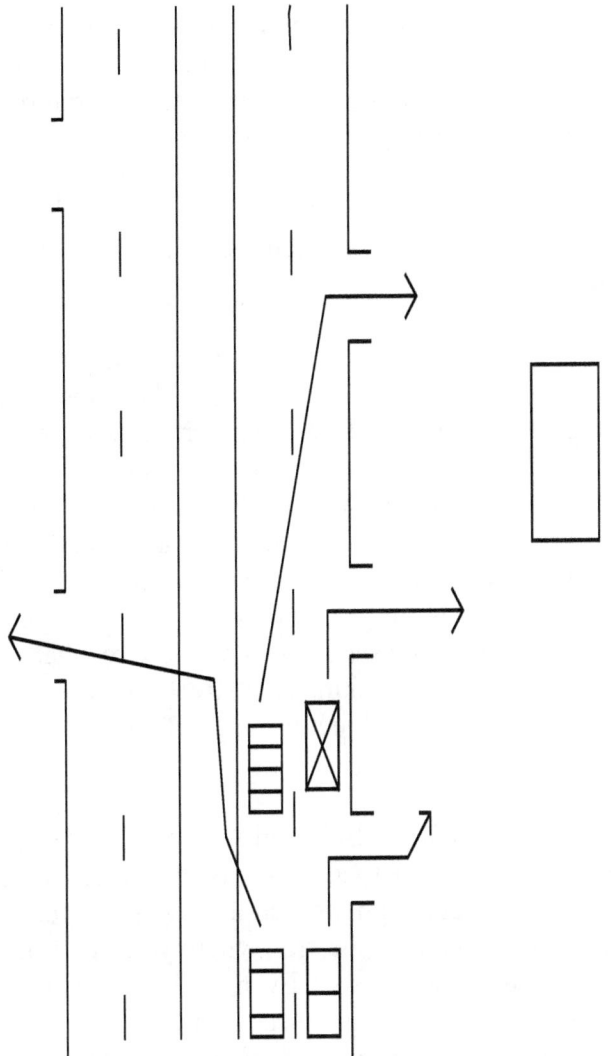

TURN-OFF WITH THREE INVESTIGATORS

Target Vehicle = Vehicle with X
Investigator # 1 = Vehicle with one line
Investigator # 2 = Vehicle with two lines
Investigator # 3 = Vehicle with three lines

In the diagram above, as the subject's vehicle (X) turns into a parking lot, investigator # 1 turns into the parking lot. Investigator #

2 proceeds by the subject and then turns away from the subject and into the parking lot across the street. Investigator # 3 passes by the target and then turns into the next entrance. A variation of this can be investigator # 1 turning into the entrance after the subject, while investigator # 2 turns into the entrance before the subject and investigator # 3 turns into the lot across the street. The investigators can take any of these positions as long as there is good communication.

When you are following subjects in a rural area, you should generally allow a greater distance between the subject's vehicle and the investigators. You *can* allow too much and go over a hill to find an intersection without knowing which way the subject turned. Which brings up another technique. Regardless of whether you are following the subject in a residential area, a rural area or on a highway, the investigator should always make it a habit to check any side streets or exit ramps that they are passing. Sometimes you can glance down just for a second and not be sure where the target is when you look up. By checking side streets as you pass them, you may be able to catch the subject turning off without being sure that they even turned.

A technique, which is also good in rural areas when there are only a few vehicles on the road, is to pass the target. Once you pass the target, continue at a higher speed until you can get to a turn-off. Hopefully, you can reach a location where you can turn off without the subject seeing you do so. Even if the target sees you turn, continue to drive slowly or go ahead and turn into a driveway and get ready to turn around after the subject passes by the intersection. You can then get back on the road behind the subject. If, however, the target happens to turn off behind you coincidentally, continue to drive ahead of the subject for a while and then turn into a driveway. Wait for the subject to pass and after several seconds, back out and continue the pursuit.

There are several variations and combinations of these techniques, however these are the basics. Switching up the vehicles that the subject sees and using these techniques is the key to not being identified and to a successful mobile surveillance.

OTHER TYPES OF SURVEILLANCE
Chapter Six

There are numerous other types of surveillances, some that are technically mobile surveillances but which deserve being discussed separately. These include using bicycles, motorcycles, three and four wheelers, boats, jet-skies, snowmobiles, R.V.'s, horses and related equipment. The investigator may start off conducting surveillance using a standard automobile and may continue to use a combination of these. A lot of the vehicles revolve around recreational uses or business related functions. In today's farming and ranching communities, it is not uncommon to observe three and four wheelers being used along with snowmobiles. In addition, hunters often use these same vehicles to get to their hunting locations.

When an investigator follows someone to a recreational area and the subject either owns or rents recreational vehicles, the investigator has to adapt. If the subject gets into a boat, chances are they are going to go somewhere away from the bank or coastline. The investigator may be able to circle the lake and locate the subjects, assuming that they stay in the same area fishing. However, if the subject decides to water-ski or just joy ride, circling the bank will probably not work. In addition, if you're at the ocean there is no bank to circle. I have been in these situations and was either fortunate enough to be able to rent a boat nearby, or I identified myself to some would-be boaters and requested their help. Obviously, you have to be careful to make sure the subjects whose help you enlist do not know the target. Although most people are more than willing to help out just for the excitement, I always try to pay them for their time and gas.

Our agency had a case in which the subject had an alleged right wrist injury. We were able to get good video of the subject using his right hand to get the boat into the water and place his fishing tackle into the boat. We knew that the subject would probably use his right hand to cast out his fishing line and wanted to get this on tape. Having followed the subject to the lake and not having a boat handy, we approached two older men who were preparing to go fishing. They were glad to get some excitement in their lives and agreed to help us out. After the subject left, we tagged along behind, leaving a good distance between the two boats and being able to use the wake (waves) left behind by the subject's boat to help us determine any changes in direction. Sure enough, the target stopped his boat in a secluded area and began to cast his fishing line, reeling it in and recasting. Due to the help of our recruited assistants, we were able to get close enough to use our zoom lenses and obtain the subject's activities on video.

Another time we observed our subject leave his house pulling a trailer with two jet skies on it. They were followed to a nearby lake where they unloaded the jet skies and began to ride them up and down the coastline. In this situation, the subjects remained close enough to the bank to allow one investigator to drive while another used the video camera. The investigators would drive along the beach or rush on ahead and park momentarily while shooting video.

Horses are another mode of transportation still used for recreation and business. Ranchers and tourist trades often use these animals and surveillance of the subject riding the horse may or may not be beneficial. Depending on the goals of the investigation, this may not be worth pursuing. However, if the subject is alleging a back injury, the jarring up and down while riding should be documented. If the subject is being observed for some other type of investigation, the goal may simply be to see what their activities are or to see where the subject goes. The investigator may be able to watch a subject on a horse if they stay parallel to a roadway. However, if they ride away from the road and towards the center of a ranch, you may have to go from mobile surveillance to foot surveillance. The subject may be able to be observed from an adjoining ranch or property. If this is the case, the investigator should use a suitable pre-text to obtain permission to be on the neighbor's property. I would not tell the neighbor the real reason you need on their ranch, but would make up some other story. For instance, you can tell them that you are a new landowner and some of your stock got out and is believed to be on their property. There are any number or stories that can be used, but definitely attempt to gain permission to be on their property. While pursuing the subject, remember to remain on the neighbor's property that you have gained authorization. Crossing onto the subject's land can leave you open for trespass charges.

In all situations in the open country, whether on water or land, the investigator should remember that sound carries a long distance in these situations. Voices, radios, pagers, cellular telephones, motors and other noises should be kept at a minimum. You should also take note of the animals the subject may have such as dogs. I can recall an incident where the subject's house could barely be observed from the road but close enough video could not be obtained from that distance. The subject exited his house and began working on the outside. We gained access from a neighbor and entered the adjoining property. After getting set up near a fence line with good brush concealment, we were able to get some good video. The subject took a break and returned inside his house. After several minutes he came back outside, this time with a German Shepherd. The dog wandered off and the next thing we knew, we saw him coming in our direction. He would stop periodically and stick his nose in the air to confirm our location. He kept coming and we were starting to get concerned when the subject noticed the dog wandering off and began to call to him. The dog stopped and spent several seconds glancing back at the subject and then in our general direction. You could tell the dog wanted to keep coming, but out of obedience, the dog turned and went back to the house. This could have very easily been a bad situation.

Following subjects in recreational vehicles can be somewhat easier if certain situations occur and your prepared for them. For instance, it is not uncommon for people who have vans, R.V.'s and related equipment to talk over the C.B. radio or low-frequency radios to friends nearby as they are driving. A good investigator should have access to a C.B and these types of radios and can scan the channels to pick up on this conversation. An investigator should also remember that if they are using these types of radios, others may be listening as well!

Cordless telephones are still often used by the target. A scanner can be purchased to listen to police calls and other frequencies. This scanner can also "scan" the airwaves and pick up cordless telephone conversations nearby the scanner. In addition to scanners, there are currently "boom" microphones and small satellite looking dishes that allow you to point them in the direction of someone and pick-up their conversations. Baby monitors are also capable of picking up wireless communications from cordless phones. These items are improving in quality, but still pick up a lot of interference and surrounding noises. It should be remembered that a person has a reasonable expectation of privacy inside their home and these items may not be legal in certain situations. However, a person out in the open, standing outside near a sidewalk may or may not be entitled to have this same expectation of privacy. Before using these types of devices, case law should be explored and legal advice obtained.

With people more and more concerned with their health, having a subject ride around on a bicycle is fairly likely. If this occurs, the investigator may be able to simply follow the subject in their vehicle. Depending on the area where the subject is riding, the investigator may have to get out on foot for better vantage points. However, in some places like New York City, there is a large work force that uses bicycles to make deliveries. If you know that your subject is involved in a situation such as this, you may have to dress the part and arrive with your bicycle and have additional investigators standing by. Adaptation is the key!

There have been times when we have had to adapt and use natural concealment. One of these involved a subject who liked to take walks in a nearby park. Being inaccessible by vehicle, we found a tall tree and scampered up the tree and set up surveillance from that point. In most jurisdictions you cannot climb into a tree and shoot video into a yard with a privacy fence but in this situation the target went to a public park. Remember, people seldom look up so in this case, being in a tree allowed the investigator to remain concealed.

On another occasion, the subject lived in a rural setting and when we passed by the house, the subject was working on a car. The road was too narrow to park on the side, even in the limited grass. The investigator, being prepared, went down the road to a nearby clearing where the vehicle could be parked and slipped into the camouflage cover-alls. The investigator then used a natural drainage ditch to crawl up closer and get in range to shoot video. In a third situation, there was a large mound of dirt built up along the side of the road opposite the subject's house. On top of this large mound of dirt were the railroad tracks. This made good concealment and the investigator came up to the tracks on foot and was able to obtain video documentation.

In a separate case, our agency used a combination of foot and mobile surveillance. The subject lived across the road from a section of land owned by the state as a right-of-way. One investigator drove just past the subject's house and slightly out of sight and stopped long enough to let the second investigator out. The investigator was able to get into the trees and vegetation across from the subject while the investigator in the vehicle waited down the road. The subject came out and worked around the yard for a while and video was obtained of this. After a period of time, the subject left in their car and the investigator in the trees was able to radio that information to the second investigator who was able to follow the subject.

If you conduct investigations very long, chances are you will follow someone to a bowling alley or a gym. If this is the case, it's time for the gym bag, unless of course you have a bowling ball handy. On one case, we had received information that the subject bowled on a league. Being prepared, I borrowed a bowling ball and bag and then carried along a separate gym bag with a couple of towels in it. Sure enough, the subject was followed to a bowling alley. I placed the camera in the gym bag and placed a towel over the camera. I then carried the gym bag and the bowling ball bag into the alley and instantly had the cover needed to pull this one off. I used the video camera in the gym bag and got what I thought was good video. However, wanting to make sure that I didn't leave without great video, I found that there was a video arcade behind the cashier. Since this was a daytime league during the week, there was no one using the video games. I was able to use the games to shelter my body and I blatantly took the video camera out and began to obtain what I was sure was good video. I concluded the surveillance and left the alley with no one being the wiser. There are now an abundance of covert camera that would work in situations such as these but the investigator must have them readily accessible and the batteries properly charged.

Then there has been numerous times when our investigators have followed subjects into a gym to workout. On several occasions, the subjects went to gyms that our investigators were already members of and getting inside was not the problem. On other occasions, we had to pose as potential clients and go through a quick sales presentation. However, before letting the sales person get too far along, we asked if we could try the facilities out and if we liked them, we could finish talking business. Of course they agree and we quickly change into workout clothes and carry the gym bag with the video camera in it and proceed to document the subject's activities. On a separate occasion, one investigator found a parking space close to the front and was able to periodically get video of the subject by shooting through the large plate glass windows while a second investigator was inside. The gym had a running track upstairs that allowed those people to look down on the first floor. The second investigator took the camera in the gym bag, sat down upstairs and acted as though they were stretching and obtained video. The point is, where there is a will, there's a way!

There are situations where you may have to get some old items from your house and sit on the side of the road with the items for sale while you are actually watching the subject. Or you can put a lawn chair out and sit down with a pad and pencil. If anyone asks, you can say that you were hired by the State to count the number of vehicles that travel the road so that a feasibility study can be completed. Using a dog as a pre-text may be useful as well. You can always take a pet for a walk which will give you the opportunity to get closer to the subject's house if need be. There are all kinds of stationary ploys that can be used in addition to these. Examples are road survey crews, telephone repairman, cable repairman, power company employee, real estate appraiser, real estate salesman, yard maintenance and a variety of others. The key to these different kinds of surveillances is remembering that no one really knows who you are and you just have to do a little acting to pull it off.

Child Welfare Cases

Surveillances involving the welfare of children are becoming more and more frequent. The question can be a moral dilemma as well as an operational dilemma for many private investigators.

Typically an ex-spouse, grandparent or other relative or custodial party will request an investigation be conducted to determine if a child is in danger. This usually means they are preparing for a custody battle. Very seldom will the court take total visitation or joint custody away from parents. They may add some conditions regarding where the child can be taken, who they can be around, supervision during visitations and similar wording. In most cases the client does not prevail or win a total victory. To prevent you from having a client that is dissatisfied, it is incumbent upon the investigator to explain this and the most likely outcome.

In these cases the client may believe or have experience with the ex-spouse abusing alcohol and/or drugs. They often want the investigator to monitor the subject, document the number of alcoholic drinks they may have and attempt to get them pulled over for Driving While Intoxicated. This may rub some PI's the wrong way but in reality, you have the duty as a private citizen to report anyone suspected of driving under the influence. In addition to the alcoholic beverages you may have observed them consume, you most likely will not know if they indulged in any prescription or illegal drugs in combination with the alcohol. It is therefore not your duty to *prove* they are under the influence. If police are successful in stopping the subject, they have the expertise and tools to make the determination. In reality, police officers are especially busy on the weekends and being able to reach the party before they get to their destination is seldom accomplished.

Emotions often cloud the client's perception and judgment in these types of case and therefore the investigator needs to have a working knowledge of family court cases. The ultimate goal of the court is to watch out for the welfare of the children. What the ex-spouse does when they are not exercising their visitation rights with the kids is irrelevant to the court. What they do when the kids are in their care and supervision is a different story. The court wants to define:

1) Who is supervising the children
2) Who is supervising the children if the parent goes to work or out to party
3) Do any of the people supervising the child present any threat

to the children
4) Are the children still attending school when with the parent
5) Is the living conditions a physical threat to the children (is the house literally falling down)

Clients normally believe that the ex-spouse is not a good parent. However, the courts are very leery of separating parents and children. Even in cases where the parent is documented having a drug abuse and alcohol abuse pattern, the court will not intercede unless there is proof the child is in danger.

Conducting surveillance around schools to determine who picks up the children and where they are taken is a logical step. However, surveillance around schools can attract the suspicions of other parents, teachers and police so you need to be ready and have an appropriate cover story. Letting someone see you raise a camera and shoot video is sure to get the police called so proper concealment of the camera is extremely important.

Like in any case, the investigator should stick to the facts and not inject any of the client's suspicions or any of the investigator's opinions. It is important for the PI to review any legal orders relating to the care and custody of the child to better understand what would be considered a violation of the court orders. Every small detail should be documented because the client may see something in the details of the video that is an issue but is not known to the PI. In these cases you should also set up a dash camera to video the driving pattern of the subject. We have documented subjects jumping curbs, medians, driving the wrong way on a one way street and similar activity. This certainly can be considered behavior that would endanger a child.

It is also advised that the investigator have wording in their contract to indicate any interference by the client terminates the contract and the retainer is forfeited. Some clients can't help but be their own worst enemy because of their emotions.

STATIONARY SURVEILLANCE
Chapter Seven

Stationary surveillance is any type of surveillance that does not involve movement and includes surveillance in vehicles, buildings, closed-circuit monitors and related activities. Although surveillance in a vehicle was covered a great deal in the chapter dealing with vehicle and mobile surveillance, the techniques surrounding stationary surveillance in a vehicle will be explained in this chapter. There are techniques that need to be developed for stationary surveillance just as there are techniques in other types of surveillance. These will be discussed in this chapter.

Stationary surveillance in a vehicle is probably one of the most boring things a person can do and is hard on your body as well. Sitting for long periods of time without being able to move and stretch is not good for the back or muscles. Unfortunately, this is part of the necessary procedures in surveillance. Finding the *proper* location to set up surveillance is probably one of the most over-looked areas of training new investigators. If the right location is obtained from the very beginning, obtaining video should not be a problem, your cover should not be compromised and the position will still allow you to follow the subject without creating problems. T.V. is once again a poor indicator of how to initiate surveillance. You will often see shows in which the investigator sits directly outside the gate to a large mansion so that when the gate opens and the car exits; the investigator's car is almost sideswiped because it is too close.

If the investigator chooses to sit on the same street that the subject's house is on, they should *never* sit closer than 10-12 houses from the subject. Even in the best of circumstances, the police may be called to check on your vehicle, which is unknown to neighbors. If this occurs and you are too close to the subject, they will possibly see the police and your concealment has just been lost. In addition, if the subject comes out and leaves in their vehicle, sitting too close will prevent you from immediately following the subject without arousing suspicions. Positioning the investigator's vehicle too close to the subject's house is probably the most abused characteristic of surveillance.

If you do choose to sit on the same street, sitting at least 10-12 houses away will allow you to identify yourself as an investigator to any suspicious neighbors. Most neighbors only have contact with the people living directly beside them or across the street. Identifying yourself to neighbor 10-12 houses away is a pretty safe bet that the subject will not even find out that an investigator is in the neighborhood. Secondly, the investigator should never identify who the subject being investigated is or where they live. In cases where the client requests surveillance and contact with neighbors to determine the subject's activities, you should not contact neighbors immediately. People are creatures of habit and history has shown that human beings have a tendency to want to talk and provide friends with exciting news. Once you talk to a neighbor, you can be sure that the subject will find out that someone is checking on them. I would suggest that you conduct at least a little surveillance before you contact neighbors and hopefully you will get lucky.

In addition to parking down the street from the subject's house, you can put up your sun visor and curtains and park between two houses. When the owners of the house come out to go to work, they will assume that the car belongs to a friend of their next-door neighbor. In addition, an investigator can park with the back end of their vehicle facing the subject's house and watch the area using the rear-view and side mirrors. If you have to identify yourself to a neighbor, you can tell them that you are an investigator and that you are watching someone down the street. Because you and your vehicle are facing away from the subject's house, the neighbor will assume that you are watching someone at the wrong end of the street. Of course, the problem with this is that you can't take you eyes off of your mirrors or the subject may leave unnoticed.

When the investigator parks down the street, this provides a safety cushion between the subject and the investigator. If the subject exits the house and begins to work in the yard, you can always move closer by waiting for the subject to turn their back momentarily. An example of the proper positioning of the investigator's vehicle in relation to the subject's house followed by the investigator moving up to a better position if needed is outlined as follows:

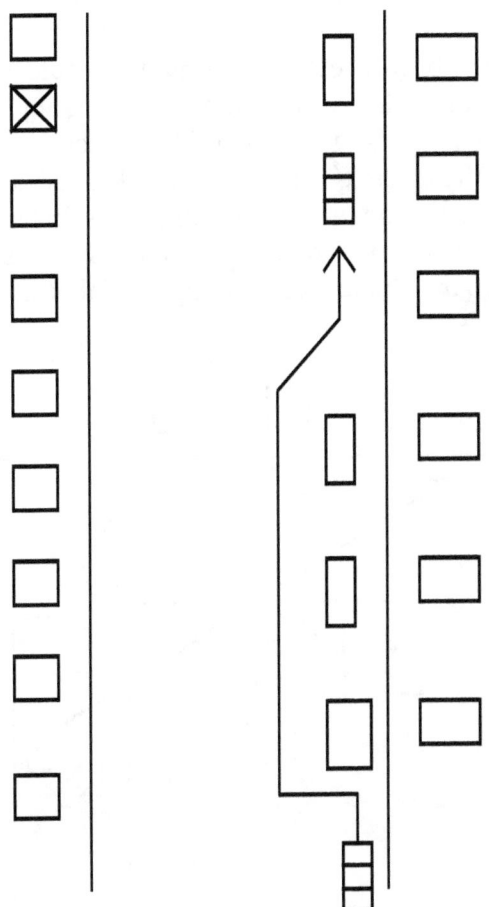

Subject's house = Square with X
Investigator = Vehicle with two lines

ORIGINAL SURVEILLANCE POSITION, MOVING CLOSER

In the diagram, the investigator parks using the other parked vehicles as concealment. Once the need arises to move closer, the investigator once again attempts to move into a position using other parked vehicles to shelter their movements.

The investigator should "canvass" the area upon arrival at a new surveillance location and check to see which directions the front of the house, the yard and the garage can be seen from. Sometimes there are bushes, trees, fences and other items that will not allow the investigator to see the house except from one end of the street. Once the front has been checked, landmarks should be obtained which will help you judge which house is the subject's house from a distance. The investigator should then check for intersections that may allow the investigator to sit on a side street and still observe the house. This is a good idea because the subject will probably not even notice you if they come out and look around or even if they drive by your vehicle. An example of this is found in the next diagram.

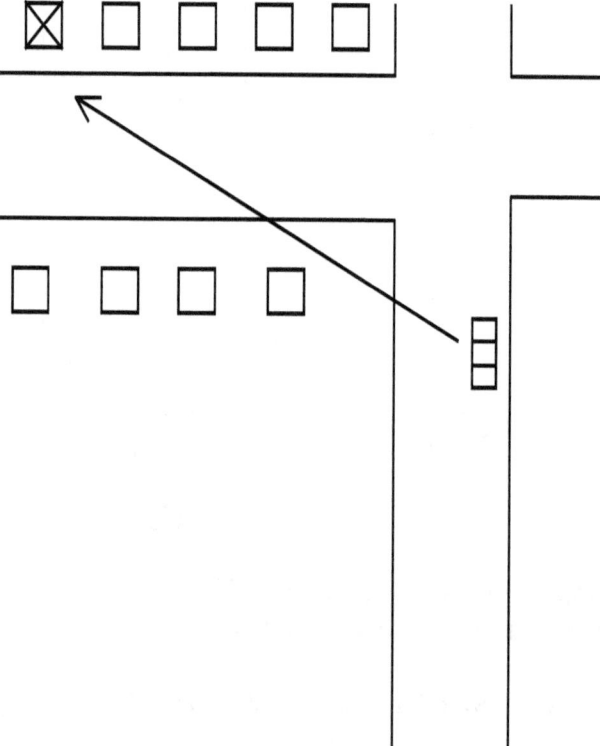

Investigator = Vehicle with two lines
Subject's House = Square with X

STATIONARY SURVEILLANCE USING AN INTERSECTION

The side streets should be explored to see if you can see the back yard of the subject's house from one of these streets. The next street to check is the street directly behind the subject's house. You may be able to sit in between houses and see the subject's back yard and carport from this location. The final street to search is the next street over from the subject's that may allow you to sit in between houses to observe the front of the subjects house and their vehicle. The investigator should be careful in these surveillance locations to make sure that the subject's vehicles and the front door can be observed. Otherwise, the subject may be able to leave in their car undetected or have a vehicle pull up in front of the house and let the subject hitch a ride. An example of this technique is as follows:

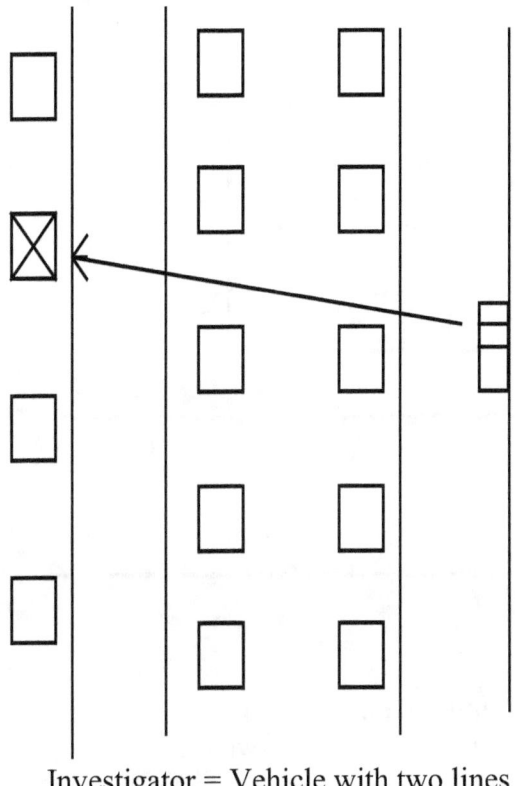

Investigator = Vehicle with two lines
Subject = House with X

SURVEILLANCE OF HOUSE FROM ONE STREET OVER

Taking advantage of side streets will also prove to be beneficial while conducting stationary surveillance. Being able to see into the backyard or the side of the house from a totally different street from the subject often poses less of a threat to you and the target. An example of the is technique is outlined in the following diagram:

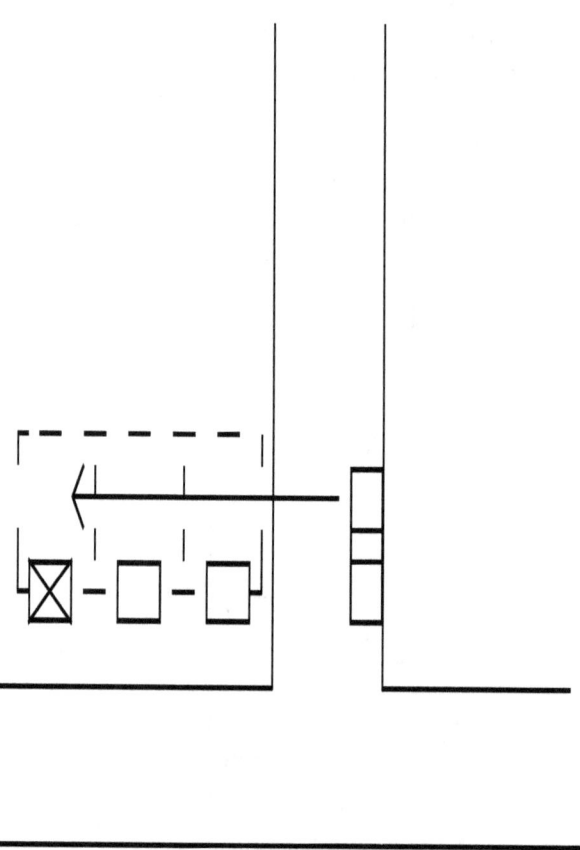

Target = House with X
Investigator = Vehicle with two lines

STATIONARY SURVEILLANCE OF BACKYARD

In this diagram, the investigator can look through the chain-link fences (dotted lines) and into the subject's backyard. This is effective and most people will not pay attention to a vehicle parked on a different street such as this and the chain link fence, trees, etc. will help distract the subject if they glance up in the direction of the investigator.

Often, it is not so much the point that an investigator's vehicle is present, but how you set up the situation to prevent suspicions. Having a vehicle that blends in with the neighborhood is the first step, which is followed by proper positioning. If the investigator gets situated early enough in the morning, putting the sun visor, curtains and other concealment in place, neighbors will think the car has been there all night. In addition, if you park your vehicle properly, each neighbor will believe that the car must belong to someone visiting their neighbor. An example of this is as follows:

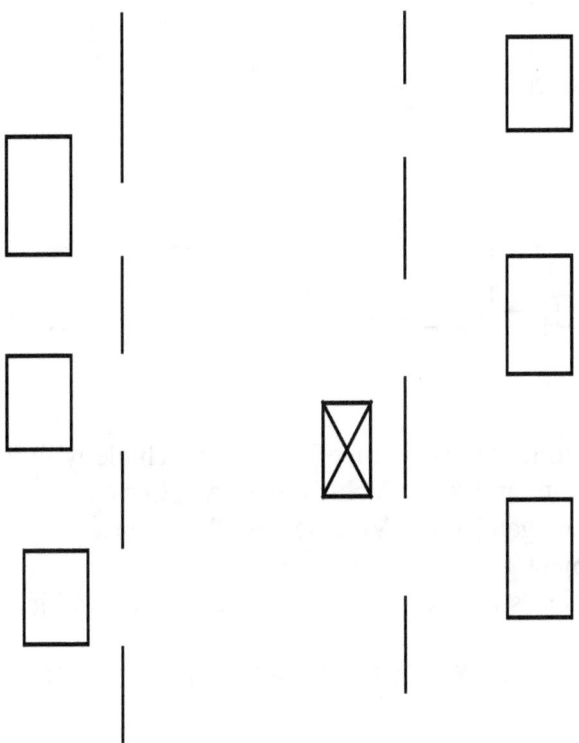

In the above diagram, the investigator (vehicle with X) is

positioned between two drive-ways to present the indication that the vehicle could be with someone visiting either neighbor.

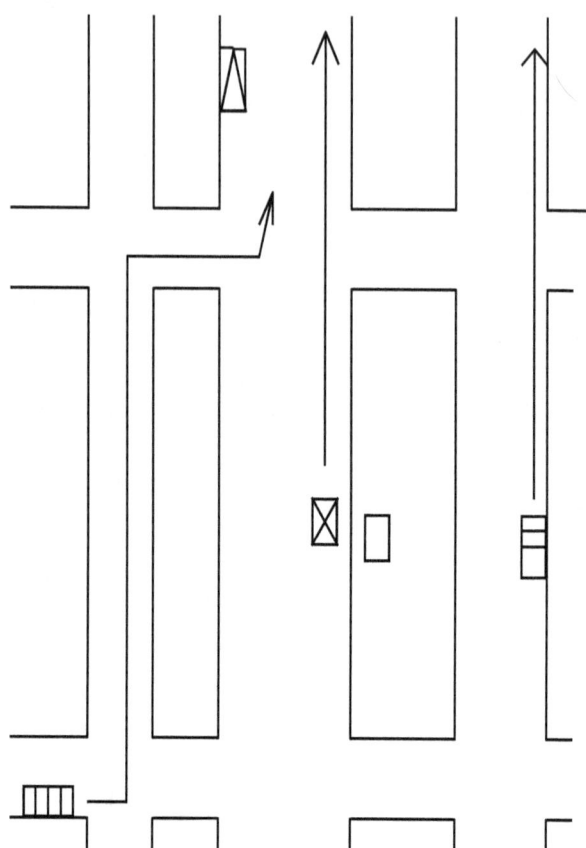

Stationary Surveillance Vehicle = Vehicle with ^
Investigator # 1 = Vehicle with two lines
Investigator # 2 = Vehicle with three lines
Subject/Target = Vehicle with X
Subject's House = Square beside subject's vehicle

STATIONARY SURVEILLANCE WITH MOBILE UNITS

There are times when a van is an appropriate vehicle. In a long-term surveillance, a van is the ideal candidate for comfort; however, they still attract too much attention from already suspicious subjects. The van can be effective however, if there are additional investigators involved in the surveillance. Once the investigator in the van determines that the subject is starting to leave the residence, communicating this to the other investigators positioned throughout the neighborhood allows the van to remain in position while the other investigations proceed with the mobile surveillance.

In the preceding diagram, the stationary surveillance van sits down the street in a safe location with good visibility of the subject's house. Investigator # 1 takes a position on the next street over to watch the backyard and also remain out-of-sight. Investigator # 2 takes a position where they can observe the opposite direction/intersection from the stationary surveillance van. Once the subject leaves the house, the investigator in the surveillance van can continue to conduct surveillance at the house or tag along at a distance and re-join the investigation when appropriate. Investigator # 1 would continue straight and run parallel to the subject, being ready to turn and take the lead position behind the subject when needed. Investigator # 2 proceeds up the street, turns and comes in behind the subject to have visual contact of the subject.

There is good, natural cover that an investigator should also take advantage of which includes a business, convenience store, small business center, office complex, park, Church or school. You can almost count on the police getting called to check you out as a suspicious person if you sit around a school and do not call the police ahead of time to let them know you'll be there. Any business or public place where there are people and other vehicles to blend into will provide good cover for stationary surveillance.

Stationary surveillance without an actual investigator is also prudent depending on the goals of the investigation and the equipment available. If the investigative agency has closed circuit equipment, the cameras can be set up to maintain observation of an area without actually having an investigator present. If you goal is to simply identify the amount of traffic, the people coming and going from a residence and similar information, this can be a beneficial method of surveillance. Typically, one investigator can position a van or similar vehicle and then adjust the camera to view the area in question. A second investigator can then pick up the first investigator. The camera can then continually record the activity, or you can utilize camera equipment that allows "snap-shots" to be taken. This means that you can set the camera to take sequences of video or photographs every 60 seconds, 5 minutes or whatever time frame you designate. There are also cameras that are only activated if a sensor observes movement. After a sufficient period of time has lapsed, the investigators can go back to the van, change tapes and continue or discontinue the investigation. This allows the greatest utilization of manpower. However, this is generally not a good method if you are concerned with the overall activity of a subject because the camera may get the subject working in the yard but no one is present to follow the subject if they drive away from the house.

There are other techniques used in stationary types of surveillance that include obtaining an adequate location for the surveillance. Some of these include using a vacant apartment. Depending on the apartment complex, the management may be more than willing to assist in an investigation and can usually be persuaded to loan an apartment to the investigators on a temporary basis. Being able to blend in with the other tenants while providing the investigators with the comforts of this environment can be very effective. If needed, investigators may also be able to persuade the leasing agent of an office complex to allow stationary surveillance to be set up in a vacant office. Of course, a vacant office has to be located in the right place to be of benefit during the investigation. However, if the investigators intend to use closed circuit cameras, a vacant office that does not offer direct observation of the subject may be suitable. The investigators will then only need limited access to the ceiling to position a camera in a hallway that will enable a closed circuit camera to observe the people coming and going.

Other methods of stationary surveillance also include positioning investigators or closed circuit cameras on the roofs of buildings, malls, schools and other related items. This allows observation from a distance without detection. However, weather can be a factor in open-air surveillance and should therefore be a consideration. When using this kind of surveillance, mobile units are usually utilized as well and are stationed in the area. One case that I was involved in utilized several investigators being positioned on the top of a large mall during the Christmas shopping season to discourage burglaries, car thefts, assaults and related activity. During our surveillance, the investigators ended up being able to spot a professional auto theft ring canvassing the mall parking lot. There were three cars involved and when the subjects found the vehicle they wanted, the passenger of one of the cars would get out and break into the vehicle while the other cars would act as cover and a source of distraction. On one occasion, the group broke into three vehicles and were preparing to leave the mall when they were stopped and detained.

One of the more conventional types of stationary surveillance is the command post centers usually found in large office buildings, industrial plants, factories and related businesses. In these situations, the business has usually spent a great deal of money installing closed-circuit cameras throughout the inside and on the exterior of the property. In addition, the business usually contracts with a security guard company or may have their own staff of security guards to patrol the grounds and to monitor the camera and TV's from a command post. However, this type of stationary surveillance is not typically done for "investigative" purposes and therefore little time will be spent discussing this topic. The main objective of this type of stationary surveillance is to deter and prevent crime and maintain the safety. These types of cameras may be beneficial, however, if an investigator is attempting to catch someone suspected of harassment or computer theft. The cameras may be able to be adjusted to pay more attention to a particular subject's activities and can pinpoint the information a subject has on a computer screen. Previous video obtained by the cameras may also be reviewed in hopes of spotting these activities through normal periodic scans of an area by the cameras.

Although there are variations of the stationary techniques discussed, the general idea is that there definitely is a place in investigations and surveillance for stationary surveillance. Usually, the best use of this method is by combining it with mobile surveillance units.

FACE-TO-FACE-CONTACT
Chapter Eight

If an investigator does surveillance for any length of time, they will be faced with many situations in which they come into contact with the subject being investigated, their relatives and friends, curious neighbors, co-workers and others who know the subject. These types of contacts can be intentional or unintentional and can be a turning point in the investigation. There may be times where approaching these subjects may be beneficial to learn more about the subject. Contact with relatives, friends and neighbors may also be conducted in an attempt to learn the actual residence of the subject, their employment or related information. When this occurs, the investigator can come away with vital information or be "blown out of the water" with their cover being disclosed.

One of the keys to face-to-face contact is to have common sense, a good story and be able to remain calm while making the subject feel comfortable with you. As an example, on one occasion, our agency was asked to conduct an investigation for a large trucking company. The client had reason to believe that one of their vice-presidents was involved in a conflict of interest and may be working as a competitor. I initiated the investigation by conducting a good background investigation where I determined that the subject did own his own trucking company and the location of the business was determined. Surveillance was conducted at this location and it was determined that the subject had several tractors, but there were no trailers observed. Over a period of three days, the subject was eventually followed from our client's office to the subject's business. He climbed into a tractor and proceeded to the client's storage area after most of the employees were gone. The subject was observed backing the tractor (with the subject's company name on it) under one of the client's trailers. It was obvious that he intended to use the client's trailer for his personal use and this was too good to pass up. Since this was in an industrial park, there were tractor-trailer rigs everywhere and observation of the subject's activities was obstructed from the road.

I knew that I would have the client's permission to be on their property, so I decided to drive onto the property, take some quick photographs and video of the subject hooking up to the trailer and then leave the lot. I obtained the documentation needed and then slowly drove out of the lot and started looking around as I drove as if I was lost. Suspecting that someone might have seen me, I had already formulated a cover story. Sure enough, I had only traveled about two blocks in the industrial park when the subject pulled up along side of me and motioned for me to roll my window down. I stopped and rolled the window down just in time to hear him say, "what are you doing taking pictures of me?" I said, "what am I doing--doing what (acting surprised) ?" He then repeated the question and I responded by stating that I was from out of town and a friend of mine who is a truck driver had a load he was hauling into the area and I was trying to find him so we could go have dinner together. The subject replied by asking what company my friend worked for. I continued by saying that he was an independent and worked for himself. The subject stated that someone had seen me taking pictures of him and he wanted to know what I was doing. Of course, I acted surprised as if I had no idea what he was talking about. Finally, I acted like a light had gone off in my mind and I replied, "oh, I know what the guy saw (as I picked up my car phone)". I told him that the guy must have seen me using the telephone because I had tried to call my friend's wife to see if she had heard from her husband in hopes that she may know where I could meet up with him. I finished the story by indicating that she had not heard from him, so I was just driving through the area trying to find his truck. The subject was satisfied with the story and began to apologize for chasing me down. Of course, I indicated that I was surprised, but no harm had been done. I was able to turn a suspicious person into a defensive, apologetic person by simply remaining calm.

Conducting investigations for insurance companies often leads to cases in which they want you to talk to neighbors to learn the activities of a subject without them knowing the real reason for the questions. I always attempt to discourage this until any surveillance that may be needed is conducted because the subject will be advised that someone was checking on them. It doesn't make any difference how good of a story you come up with, neighbors will use this to create a bond and further a relationship. They may only say something like, " a guy called the other day doing a background check for the job you applied for", but this is all that is needed to alert the subject since he probably didn't apply for a job. There are numerous pre-text forms of questioning, but being able to guide the conversation into a situation that will allow you to ask personal questions about a neighbor is difficult.

There are times when you have to take chances and make contact with subjects like leasing agents at apartment complexes. Every once in a while, the information you are able to turn up provides you with the subject's address, but not the apartment number. Checking utility records, license plates and other records just does not give you the apartment. When this occurs, the investigator may be forced into talking to the apartment's leasing agent. Once again, an investigator should be ready for the unexpected. I had another case in which this very situation presented itself. My client, an attorney, had requested surveillance on the subject to determine if the injuries they alleged were consistent with the subject's activities. I had been unable to locate the subject's apartment number, so I took a chance and entered the leasing agent's office for the complex. As I entered, I observed one female sitting behind a desk and another female sitting in a chair on the other side. Through the brief conversation that I over-heard, the subjects were obviously friends. I waited for the pair to stop speaking and hoped that the one female would go ahead and leave the office. Unfortunately, she didn't and this was a small office with no other offices to ask the leasing agent to step in.

I indicated that I needed to locate the apartment number for my subject (who was a female) and that all I had was the address for the complex. The leasing agent asked the name of the person I needed to contact. In a split second, the thoughts ran through my mind that I should give her a bogus name and try again with another investigator, but then decided to take a chance. I blurted out the subject's name and the leasing agent replied by stating, "your in luck, this is her (pointing to the other lady)". I couldn't believe it; I had done the last thing I wanted to do by coming face-to-face with the subject. I quickly thought of a suitable excuse and indicated that I was there *on behalf* of XYZ Insurance Company and that they were concerned that she was not getting her checks. I further indicated that they had reason to believe that she was not getting the checks and that someone may be forging her name to them. She replied by saying, "you know, I just called my attorney this morning because I haven't received my last two checks". I took a sigh of relief and then assured her that everything would be done to correct the situation. I then left, called the insurance adjuster and advised them of the situation and then waited down the street for the subject to leave. After about 5 minutes, she left the office and proceeded to her apartment. I now knew the apartment number and reassigned the case to another investigator to finish. This is another example of how keeping your cool can prevent disaster.

I have found that when conducting surveillance in a neighborhood, you have to sit far enough away from the subject's house to prevent being detected. Another reason is because suspicious neighbors may call the police on a vehicle and/or person that they don't recognize. The investigator should be well versed in the proper etiquette when approached by police officers. The investigator has to identify themselves as a private investigator; however, the client-confidentiality should be adhered to. Depending on the situation, I may or may not tell the officer who is being investigated. In smaller communities, the officer will probably know something about the subject and may be able to supply you with some good leads. However, you may run into a situation like I did. On one occasion, I was sitting about two blocks away from the subject's house when the officer arrived. I tried to be polite and even went out of my way to initiate some meaningful conversation. Being a former police officer, I knew how to deal with this situation. The officer went through the normal identification procedures and then kept coming back to the question of who was being investigated. I attempted to graciously pass over the question. The officer kept coming back to the same question, which made me a little uneasy. I was just about to give in and tell the officer when I looked down at the nametag on his uniform. The officer had the same last name as the subject being investigated, which in itself would not have been a big issue since it was a fairly common last name. Due to the officer's persistent questioning though, I decided not to tell the officer and he finally left the area. I then made a couple of calls to some friends on the police department and discovered that the officer was the brother of the subject being investigated. Luckily this is not the norm. All in all, the officers can be a big help, but an investigator should know their legal boundaries and follow gut instincts in this type of situation.

A good habit to get into when you observe a marked police unit turning onto the street in which you are conducting surveillance is to get your badge and P.I. identification out. As the officer passes by your vehicle, they are sizing the situation up and assessing any threat that you may present. When the officer gets close enough, hold the badge and identification up in plain view. This will cause the officer to approach you in a better attitude and will help set the ground rules for the conversation because you have been thoughtful of the officer's situation. If the officer comes up from behind, simply roll the window down and hold the badge and identification case against the outside of the car door with the badge facing the officer. You may also be able to hold the badge up inside the vehicle to alert the officer to your identification. Whatever the means, you should make an attempt to make the contact a source of minimal tension for you and the officer.

Another reason for doing your homework before approaching neighbors is because you may be knocking on a relative's door. If the investigator would do some preliminary background searches, they will know this and be able to prevent a big mess. Contact with neighbors, or for that much, anyone involves setting the groundwork. You have to approach them in a non-aggressive manner while being aggressive enough to dominate the situation. For the most part, people like to talk. Therefore, a good investigator only has to prompt the person to make them begin to converse. There may be times when the person even states right up front that they do not want to get involved and that they will not tell you anything about their neighbors. Simply acknowledge their statement and then keep talking. Try to access the situation and find something that will obviously cause the person to keep talking. For instance, if you see photographs of the person's children, make a comment about how nice they look. All parents like to receive comments concerning their children. You may see a photograph of someone in a military uniform, cheerleader's outfit or similar uniforms that will present a good opportunity for conversation. If you are talking to a person who lives out in a rural area, inquire about how the farming season is progressing. It doesn't take much effort to engage in conversation and by doing this, you put the person at ease and win their confidence. After they accept you and are comfortable with you, the investigator can then tie the conversation back into the original questions.

The investigator should always remember that sitting in a neighborhood appears to be an aggressive action to the neighbors because they do not know you or what your intentions are. With the increase in crime, neighbors are sticking closer together and watching out for one another. Be sensitive to this and when a neighbor approaches, be courteous. The typical questions when approached by a neighbor will be, "can I help you?", or "are you lost?". I have seen investigators who when asked, can I help you; respond by simply stating "no" without any additional conversation. All investigators feel like doing this because we get tired of curious neighbors, however, by doing this, you may create a hostile neighbor when they could just as easily be an asset. Remember that the neighbor who approaches you with this type of inquiry is really asking, "are you a criminal, are you here for a good reason or is someone in trouble". This is the neighbor's attempt at a pre-text line of questioning and the investigator should respect the person and respond accordingly.

There will be times when a neighbor just simply doesn't like the idea of your being on their street "snooping". They may even tell you that you can't sit in front of their house. When this occurs, simply tell the subject that it is not against the law to sit in a parked car that is legally parked and that you pay taxes and have the right to sit on the street. You may continue by advising them that it is not your intention to make them uncomfortable and that they should look at you as an extra source of security sense you will be observing the entire street. If they continue in this manner, it may be advisable to adjust your surveillance position to minimize any hostility in the area.

Then there are the neighbors that can be an asset. They will allow you to sit in their driveway of their house and conduct surveillance. These types of people can almost be too helpful because they want to be involved and know everything that is going on. The investigator has to include them in the situation enough to keep them useful, but not enough to let them get in the way or possibly get hurt.

Approaching family members is probably one of the most difficult situations for obvious reasons and should be discouraged unless as a last resort. On one occasion, I had to conduct surveillance on a subject in a rural area. The house sat on a couple of acres of land with three other houses close-by. I had not been able to find any information concerning which house was actually the one my subject was living in. The houses were positioned in a manner that caused observation of the vehicles to be impossible unless on the dirt road directly beside the houses. The road was a long road that dead-ended into a gate. It had been raining and the fields all around the house were muddy and I would have gotten stuck if I had tried to venture off the road. I decided to drive down the road and look as though I was lost, taking enough time to get the vehicle license plates. I had just accomplished this and was getting ready to back-up down the road when a pick-up truck pulled in behind me. A male subject stopped his vehicle directly behind me giving me nowhere to go. The driver of the truck exited the vehicle and got out with a threatening tone of voice and demanded, "what do you want"? I told the subject that I needed to speak to my subject. He replied, that's my son. It was one of those situations where you knew you had better think quickly.

I knew that the subject/target had been in a bar-room fight with another guy who lived nearby. I quickly thought and came up with a story. I indicated that the other subject involved in the fight with his son was trying to sue the bar and I needed to get his son's story as to what really happened. The father, knowing that his son had been involved in the fight, let his defense down. After a brief conversation, the father advised that his son was down the road about a mile working on a tractor that had broken down. I thanked the subject and then proceeded down the road to find my subject. I was able to get some great video of the subject and then approached him with the same story to make things look good. Once again, keeping a cool head allowed me to remain safe and I was able to conclude the investigation successfully.

Contacting relatives is hard to do when trying to use a pre-text because they know the subject real well and will probably be able to determine quickly as to whether or not you appear to be legitimate. If all else fails, you can try the old stand-by cover story that you work as a credit collector and you are sure that their relative is not the subject your after, but you have to check out all your leads. The potential stories are endless, but the ability to pull them off depends on the cool, collective manner in which the investigator works.

As a cautionary note, there are laws that prohibit you from acting like the party in question. You cannot pre-text a financial institution and inquire about "your" account when in fact you are not the person who has the account.

It is always good for a PI to have documents that support the pre-text. I have professionally printed business cards and websites for my undercover name. You should develop a name and quasi-identity for your undercover personality. It should be a name that you would actual answer to if someone called out to you. The job, city you live in and general personality characteristics should all be something that you can pull off.

OUT-SOURCING
Chapter Nine

If a person works as a P.I. for very long, they will have to confront the use of out-sourcing. To say it another way, the investigator will have to assign a case to another investigator in a different part of the country. This sounds reasonably easy, but keep in mind that not all investigators are good at surveillance.

I remember a case in which a good client of mine asked us to conduct an investigation in a different part of the State. I asked him if he wanted us to travel there, or if he wanted us to supervise another agency's work. The client said that either way would be all right with him. Due to a heavy caseload and my investigators all being tied up, I decided to assign the case to another firm. I made some calls and several colleagues referred me to the same company, which was a nation-wide, well known company. This company is known primarily as a supplier of security guards, but does have an investigation department.

I was real careful when making the assignment to ask the right questions and make sure that they understood what we needed. I asked them if they were equipped to conduct surveillance and they indicated they had the standard equipment. In addition, the manager stated that they do quite a bit of surveillance. The investigation was about 50 miles outside of a major metropolitan area. Before the end of the conversation, I confirmed our understanding. I made sure that we did not want to be charged for renting a video camera, for hotel expenses, and for any background information, which we had already conducted and supplied to their office. The investigation was limited to $2,000 and we knew that the subject was going to be moving over the up-coming weekend. All they had to do was to show up and get video of the subject moving furniture to prove the subject wasn't hurt as they claimed.

On the following Monday, I walked in to find a report that they had faxed to my office. The investigator indicated that he watched the subject move every conceivable piece of furniture over the Saturday and Sunday before, but failed to get any video or photographs. In addition, there was a bill for $3,000 that accompanied the report. The bill listed items such as "video rental", hotel room expense and background investigation expense. I called the investigator up, thinking there must be some mistake. The investigator went on and on about all the things the subject was observed lifting. When I asked the question, "did you get it on video", the investigator replied, "no, but I can testify in court as to what I saw". To make matters worse, he indicated the charges on the bill were not incorrect.

I promptly gave the investigator a crash course in business, referring him to the assignment sheet that I had faxed to their office after our conversation. I told the investigator that no one cares what he can testify to, as a picture *is* worth a thousand words. The guy knew he had stepped in it and agreed to go back out that day free of charge to see if he could get any video of the subject finishing up the moving. The following day the investigator called up all happy and joyful because he had gotten some video of the subject outside moving a chair and table. Then came the bombshell. He said, "oh, by the way, while I was filming the subject, you will see on the video where he came up to me and asked me why he was being filmed". An additional bill for $1,200 followed this conversation up. Before it was all over, their attorneys were talking to my attorneys about why I wouldn't pay the $4,500 bill instead of just the $1,000. Their company finally backed off and accepted the agreed upon $1,000.

This is just one example of some of the poor results I have experienced while out-sourcing cases. I have developed some good contacts over the years and do not hesitate to use them, but I am very skeptical of assigning any cases to an agency I don't know.

If a P.I. decides to out-source an investigation, the investigator should make contact with several organizations that serve as a referral base for investigators. One of these is the National Association of Investigative Specialists located in Austin, Texas. A second source is the ION network in Tempe, Arizona. Another good source is to check with the Risk Manager for the largest city in the area that you need the surveillance done. Often, the risk managers know of good investigators since they normally hire investigators on cases involving city matters. I would also recommend you contact the association for the state in question (ex: Texas Association of Licensed Investigator) as many have membership lists that can be searched by geographic location or specialization.

Once the agency is determined, the P.I. making the assignment should telephone their office and ask questions concerning the type of work that they specialize in and their equipment. In addition, the P.I. should have some type of assignment sheet that will provide the firm who is doing the investigation with all of the facts, details, guidelines, requirements, specific instructions and the amount of monetary expenditures agreed upon. The agency making the assignment should also make sure the other agency has the appropriate licenses and insurance coverage. It is then the P.I. who makes the assignments responsibility to manage and supervise the case. The P.I. should make periodic contact with the other investigator to keep up-dated on the progress of the case and to suggest additional activity. All of these things may not keep a bad investigation from passing through, but it will sure help to decrease the odds.

A P.I. who is attempting to make an out-source assignment should also recognize that there are other factors that may be an issue. I have found investigators who attempt to project a "bigger" look by showing that they have offices all over the place. Some of these may be legitimate, however, a great many are actually affiliates or franchises. The P.I. making the assignment should be aware of this because the actual company may not have a great deal of supervision over an affiliate or their product. Often, an affiliate will operate under their own name, as well as the affiliate's name. I have found that the agencies operating under their own name may not have that good of a reputation, but the affiliate name gives them more creditability. Then there are those agencies that put a telephone in another agency's office across the State. That way, when the telephone rings, it can be answered as if they actually had an office at that location.

Some P.I. firms also are known for using mainly part-time employees. The problem with this is that they are normally only after a paycheck and don't have a great deal of loyalty and may not care too much about the success of the investigation, just as long as they get paid. I know of one firm who advertises that they are nationwide, but actually rely on part-timers for the majority of the areas covered. These kinds of techniques can create confusion and a poor work product.

I have also attempted to call some of the agencies that have large advertisements in the yellow pages. Some of these have no one answering their telephones during normal working hours, or they may use an answering machine or answering service. This is something else that needs to be taken into account because you may not want to make an assignment to an agency that is hard to get a hold of. Another good idea is to require the investigator being assigned an out-sourcing case to have to shoot 30-45 seconds of video every 30 minutes, even if nothing is happening. If you get a report and video with no activity, at least you know the guy was there instead of out working two or three cases at the same time. Insurance companies have SIU's (special investigative units) that deal primarily with vendors who conduct investigations on their behalf. These SIU's have gotten very good at supervising their vendors. As a P.I., we will also have to adapt to this as well unless the decision is made to not out-source.

Early on in my career, I made the decision to do as little out-sourcing as possible. However, circumstances happened that required me to re-think this approach. On one case, we were watching a guy who had an insurance claim and we obtained video of him putting suitcases in the trunk of his car. We began to follow the subject in the direction of the airport and as we got closer, we called the client. After discussing the possibilities, the client requested that we not leave the area with the subject but attempt to determine where he was going and get an investigator on the other end to pick him up.

Sure enough, the subject went to the airport and we followed him inside to the ticket counter. Thankfully, the flight was going to a city that we knew the subject was born in and therefore assumed he was going to visit relatives. We scrambled back to our office and began to hunt down a good investigator who was available on the spur of the moment. Fortunately, we located one and they turned out to be very good at surveillance. The investigators picked the subject up at the other end and followed the subject for two days, getting good video that was used by the client to help settle the case.

If you are going to accept cases from other PI's as well as out-source cases to other investigators, you should offer a professional discount off of your hourly rate. You can bill your normal rate, pay the PI doing the work the negotiated discounted rate and you both can make some money. Some prefer just to hand the case off to the other PI or to hand it off and accept a referral fee. You should remember that the client came to you because of your reputation and you have expenses related to marketing and obtaining new clients.

The decision has to be made early on as to whether or not your agency will out-source. There are certain risks that come with the use of out-sourcing, but as a whole, out-sourcing can assist a P.I. if used right.

WRITING THE REPORT
Chapter Ten

Conducting surveillance is just one part of the over-all process of supplying a service to a client. Although it is a good business practice to provide a verbal update to most clients, a written report should follow-up the completion of the investigation unless prior instructions have been given. The report should be easy to follow, concise, well written and should follow a logical sequence. The report should include copies of any pertinent records, photographs of other documents.

There is no single-form of report writing, however, some are better than others. I have often heard my clients state that they have gotten reports from other investigators who were obviously police officers because of the choppy sentences and slang that was used in the reports. I have even seen investigators who turn in a hand-written report in pencil. The investigator should remember that this is the final product, which is the product that will leave a lasting impression with the client. This is the perfect opportunity to further demonstrate your professionalism and further market your services. Depending on the client, you may want to place the report in attractive binders that may even have your company name and logo on it. Some clients do not require this, such as the typical insurance case. The insurance adjusters have files with the two-prong holders in the file jackets. Although my agency used to supply all reports to out clients in the nice report covers, the adjusters started to return the covers to my office. They indicated that they took the documents out, punched holes in the top and placed the reports in the file with the rest of the documents. However, in most other cases, presentation is very important. We have all heard that first impressions are lasting impressions, so the investigator should make every attempt to present their product well.

After talking to other investigators, seeing reports from other agencies and talking with my clients, it appears that there are two schools of thoughts when it comes to reports. The first school of thought seems to be that a report should be as short as possible with limited details. The other school of thought is a report that goes into great detail. I have often heard investigators make statements like, "who cares what color of house the guy lives in", and "what difference does it make what streets he took to get there"? Depending on your client, this may or may not be true. A lot of insurance adjusters want this kind of information because they are not out in the field and they use this to get a mental picture of their claimant to see if it fits with other information they have obtained.

I require my investigators to provide a detailed report for several reasons. It is common to have a client call up and request additional surveillance. If the case gets assigned to someone other than the original investigator, this information can come in handy. I have seen investigators who have followed up a previous investigation and lost the subject while tailing them. If the first investigator listed the streets and locations that the subject traveled, the other investigator can use this information to re-trace the subject and we have found numerous subjects using this method. In addition, the investigator has to remember that the one representative who asked you to conduct the investigation may not be the only one to review the report. It is not uncommon for an adjuster to preview the report, followed by their supervisor, their attorney, rehabilitation nurses, doctors and other persons. What is unimportant to one subject may be of benefit to another. As a key, it is usually better to supply too much information than not enough.

The basic report format should include several headings that should include re-stating the client's request and the objectives of the investigation. The next topic should include a summary of the investigation, the details of any record checks, the details of any surveillance and a conclusion. The body of the report should be written in easy to read sentences. Sample reports have been enclosed for guidance:

SAMPLE REPORTS:

CLIENT OBJECTIVE:

The XYZ Investigative Company was contacted by Mr. Don Smith of the ABC company on January 1, 2013. Mr. Smith asked the investigator to determine the criminal history of Jack Johnson and to determine Mr. Johnson's activities on Friday, January 5, 2013.

REPORT SUMMARY:

The investigation was completed on time and on the day as requested by the client. A check of local records revealed Mr. Johnson has one arrest conviction on file for DWI. The surveillance resulted in the subject being followed as he took his kids to school, continued to the grocery store and then returned home. Later in the day, Mr. Johnson was observed chopping firewood and stacking the timber. The investigation was terminated at 5:00 P.M. as the client had specified.

DETAILS OF RECORDS SEARCH:

The investigator conducted a search of the County Criminal records for the years of 1988 until the present. The records indicated one match on file involving Mr. Johnson. Case # 95-12343, filed May 5, 2005, revealed that subject was arrested and pleads guilty to DWI, receiving a one-year probation and $450 fine.

DETAILS OF SURVEILLANCE:

7:00 A.M.: The investigator established the surveillance on Friday, January 5, 2013 at the residence of Mr. Johnson. The address, 134 Oak Circle, is on the north side of town and the house is a two-story brown wood structure that sits on two acres of land. There were two vehicles present that included a red 1995 Ford truck and a green 1994 Ford Tempo that are both registered to Mr. Johnson. Several lights were observed on inside the house. No activity was observed outside the residence.

7:45 A.M.: A subject believed to be Mr. Johnson exited the residence wearing blue jeans, a long-sleeve blue shirt and appeared to be 40-45 years old, average build and had glasses. The subject got into the Ford truck and started the engine to allow it to warm up. After 1-2 minutes, two kids exited the house and got into the truck. One child appeared to be 10-12 years old and was a male. The other child was a female and appeared to be 14-15 years old.

7:48 A.M.: The three subjects left in the truck, turned right onto Hwy. 123 north-bound, turned left and continued west on Constitution, left on Independence and stopped in front of Johnson Middle School. Both of the kids exited the truck and entered the school. Mr. Johnson then continued back to Hwy. 123 and traveled south to the Westlawn exit where he parked and entered a grocery store.

8:45 A.M.: Mr. Johnson was observed pushing a grocery cart from the store to his truck and he placed three sacks of groceries into the truck. Video documentation was obtained of this activity.

8:49 A.M.: Mr. Johnson left the store in his truck and took Hwy. 123 back to his residence. Upon arrival, video documentation of the subject taking the groceries into the house was obtained.

11:15 A.M.: The mailman delivered mail to the subject's residence.

11:35 A.M.: A female believed to be Mrs. Johnson, was observed retrieving the mail.

1:00 P.M.: Mr. Johnson was observed exiting the back door of the residence and walking almost 100 feet to a stack of logs. Mr. Johnson began to use an ax to chop the logs into smaller pieces. After completing this task, Mr. Johnson then stacked the logs up and carried several armloads into the house. Video documentation was obtained of this activity.

2:15 P.M.:   Mr. Johnson completed his tasks and returned into the house.

3:00 P.M.:   Mrs. Johnson left in the Ford Tempo and returned at 3:20 P.M. with the two kids.

5:00 P.M.   Contact was made with the client who asked that the investigation be terminated.

CONCLUSION:

The investigation was completed as requested by the client. Mr. Johnson was observed to be active as noted in the video documentation. The client may consider additional surveillance in the near future to better document the subject's activities.

SECOND REPORT EXAMPLE:

REQUEST OF CLIENT

On January 3, 2013, Mrs. Julie Robertson, a representative of the Affordable Rates Insurance Company requested XYZ Investigative Agency to conduct an investigation in reference to Mr. John Johnson. The client requested that the subject be observed to determine any physical limitations that may be present due to an automobile accident occurring with their insured on December 3, 1995. A check of Mr. Johnson's driving history was also requested.

SUMMARY OF FINDINGS

A check of the Driver's License records revealed that Mr. Johnson has two prior accidents and two speeding tickets on file. The surveillance resulted in the claimant being observed playing basketball, working in a construction related job and running several errands. The video documentation demonstrates that the claimant is capable of leading a productive life-style without indications of physical limitations.

DETAILS OF RECORDS

The State Driving History records were researched and several listings were found to be associated with the claimant and are as follows:

- A) 12/3/05   Motor Vehicle Accident
- B) 09/31/05 Speeding 70-55
- C) 07/22/05 Motor Vehicle Accident
- D) 10/12/06 Speeding 50-40

DETAILS OF SURVEILLANCE

The XYZ Investigative Agency initiated the surveillance on January 5, 2013 at 7:30 A.M. by locating the claimant's residence, 146 Redwood Dr. The house is a red brick one-story structure with a two-vehicle garage. There was a chain link fence around the back yard and there was a boat parked in the back yard. Upon arrival, no vehicles were observed outside of the garage and no activity was observed.

At 7:45 A.M., the right garage door opened electronically and a blue and white 1982 Ford Ranger with license # 452-BNH, which is registered to the claimant, backed out. A light blue Honda Accord was observed inside the garage briefly as the garage door closed. A white male subject who appeared to be the claimant was observed driving the truck. The subject left the subdivision, turned left on Main, right on Green St., continued on Hwy. 183 and exited at Smith Rd. The subject pulled into the parking lot where a new mall is being built next to the highway. The claimant exited the truck, obtained a tool belt out of the truck and walked to the construction sight. The claimant was observed as he helped carry lumber, climbed ladders, used an electric circular saw and a hand saw and performed other related functions. Video was obtained of this activity.

At 11:30 A.M., the subject left in his truck and proceeded to a nearby convenience store where he purchased a sandwich and a drink and sat in his truck eating. The claimant returned to the construction sight at 12:35 P.M. and once again began to perform construction related tasks. The claimant carried several large bags that appeared to weigh 40-50 lbs. and carried a bucket in one hand as he climbed a ladder. Once again, video documentation was obtained of this activity.

At 5:15 P.M., the claimant returned to his truck and took the same route back to his residence. Upon arrival, the garage door opened electronically and the truck was pulled into the garage. The claimant exited the truck and entered the house. Surveillance was discontinued at 6:00 P.M.

Surveillance was resumed at the claimant's house the following Saturday at 9:00 A.M. There were no vehicles observed outside of the garage and no activity noted upon arrival. At 10:30 A.M., the claimant exited the garage in the Ford truck and proceeded just down the road to Campbell Elementary School. The claimant joined three other male subjects and they engaged in a 3 on 3-basketball game. Video documentation of this activity was obtained.

At 12:15 P.M., the claimant left the school and continued to the EZ convenience store on Apple Rd. where he purchased a drink. The subject then continued to the Get Clean Dry Cleaners on Hwy. 183 where he picked up several items. The claimant then returned to his residence. Surveillance was discontinued at 3:00 P.M.

CONCLUSION

The investigation revealed that the claimant is active and is capable of continuing to work at a physically strenuous job. In addition, the subject was observed engaging in a basketball game and running several errands. The client may wish to consider additional surveillance as the weather gets warmer as the claimant has a boat in his back yard and may engage in water related sports.

Many investigators are now going to a paperless case management system. These allow the investigator(s) to post their notes daily. When the investigation is complete, a report on your pre-set letterhead can easily be generated. You can also track your expenses and create invoices from the case management system. Your clients can also log in to the site and review notes along the way. One of the best reasons to use a paperless case management system is so you will not have to deal with boxes and boxes of old files that need to be destroyed at some point.

There is no right and wrong way to write a report, as long as it is professional and provides the details needed for the client to properly evaluate the investigator's work and the facts in the case. The who, what, when, where and how should always be outlined for the report to be correct. With today's computers, spell check capabilities and laser printers, there is no reason why a client should not get a report that is professional in content and appearance.

MARKETING YOUR COMPANY
Chapter Eleven

It doesn't make any difference how good you are at surveillance if no one knows about it. I have seen several police officers retire from the department and immediately start their own P.I. firm, just to go out of business just as quickly. Sometimes, the idea of being in business is more impressive than actually doing the things that have to be done to get and keep business.

I often see police officers who decide to start their own business with the promise from one or two attorneys who say they will give them business. If these attorneys are a sole practitioner or in a small firm, they may give you all their business (all 3-4 cases a month). This typically will not support an investigator.

The first thing an investigator has to decided is what market(s) they going to specialize in. Most agencies have a specialty such as locating people, background investigations, surveillance, insurance cases, law firm work, corporate work and similar cases. The market that you target will depend on how to approach these clients.

For example, if you decide to go after work from lawyers, decide which kind of lawyers. Are they going to be plaintiff lawyers (those who bring lawsuits against others on behalf of their clients) or defense lawyers (those who defend others being sued). Or you may decide to go after cases from attorneys who do criminal cases. The first thing you should do is to call directory assistance and see if there is a local chapter of attorneys such as the San Antonio Bar Association. You then need to find out if the association publishes a book listing each local attorney, which will give their type of expertise, address, etc... Obtain one of these and use it to market the attorneys who handle the cases that best fit with your own expertise.

The best way to get your foot in the door is to call up the law firm and ask to speak to the office manager. Introduce yourself and your company, keeping it brief. Ask them if they would mind if you mailed them your marketing information and follow-up with a call in a week or so. Once you mail the information, give it sufficient time to reach their office and then call them again. Refresh their memory concerning your last conversation and ask to schedule an appointment to meet with them. Remember that time is money to an attorney, so make sure that you let them know it will only take 10-15 minutes. You now have a foot in the door and the rest is up to you.

While talking to the bar association, you may inquire about advertising rates and if they publish a monthly newsletter than you may also be able to advertise in. If you are good at speaking, you may inquire about being a guest speaker at one of their meetings.

If you decide to go after a different profession, such as insurance companies, you can do the same as with attorneys. Call and find out the number to the local claims association, obtain one of their books and use it for marketing. You may also check with the State in which you are licensed as a P.I. and found out from the State Board of Insurance what is required to be able to teach continuing education courses for insurance adjusters. If you can qualify, this is a good marketing tool. The thing to be careful of when being a guest speaker such as this is to not over-sale yourself. Let your speaking and the expertise demonstrated in your speaking market for you. No one likes to have anyone stand up and do nothing but tell how great they are in comparison to their competitors. That's not why they are there. Take a moment to tell them who you are, how you can help them and then move on to the topic of the speech. If you present yourself well, you will receive cases from them.

Another good method of marketing any professional is to invite them to lunch. Some companies have strict policies against their employees engaging in this, however, it is a good method if you can use it. Once you have someone away from the pressures of their office, enjoying good company and a good meal, your message will be better received and understood.

If you decide to go after the domestic (divorce) cases, you should take advantage of local newspapers that are free to the general public. A good size advertisement in this type of newspaper will usually run about $50 per week. In addition, you should consider marketing the attorneys that handle these types of case. Another good source of advertisement is to put business cards or flyers on the bulletin boards of courthouses, restaurants, and similar places.

Other avenues of advertising may include military base newspapers, credit union newsletters, fraternal organization newsletters, bars, clubs and similar examples that will not cost a great deal to advertise.

If the targeted clients are a type of profession that have weekly or monthly meeting, find out if they are open to vendors. If they are, go and "meet and greet". Sure I know, you have surveillance that needs to be conducted. But taking the time to mix with your clients and potential clients is one of the ways to keep you busy.

Another source of marketing in the local Chamber of Commerce. Join this and you will be sure to start meeting the business community on their level. Most Chambers offer more events than any one-person can possibly go to. However, this is a good source of marketing.

Once you get an audience with a potential client, remember that appearance is everything. I know of one investigator that dressed like he was a throwback to the 60's with long hair, worn-out jeans and a T-shirt. He told his clients that he marketed his clients like that to show them how well he can fit in at some of the lower-class establishments. Needless to say, the clients weren't impressed. By nature, people want to be around other people who appear successful. Have your marketing speech well thought out, concise and as short as possible. Clients like to hear all the "war-stories", but they also want to get to know the person that they are dealing with. Take time to cultivate this relationship and it will be a strong one for years to come.

Once you tell the client how great you are and how well you communicate with them, show them. There is nothing worse for the PI industry than to have an investigator tell how great they are and then once they get assigned a case, take 2-3 months to get it done and to not keep the client updated. Make an effort to update the client at least once a week, either verbally or through a quick fax that is short and to the point.

Another good example of marketing is putting out a company newsletter. Sure this takes time and costs a lot in postage, but it is one of those methods that keeps your name in front of the client. Using only telephone contact and mailing marketing material gets old after a while. Learning to keep you name in front of them as a silent reminder is a good technique. Besides a newsletter, you can drop off some donuts with a card taped to the box, you can drop off some pens with your name on them or send them a card at Christmas. These are just the little extras that will keep you where you need to be with a client.

Just as a good investigator takes field notes, so should a good marketing person. Each time you call a client or potential client, take a moment to write a brief summary of the statement. Often, you may get a message indicating the client is out on vacation, sick leave or at a seminar. The next time you call, this can be a source of starting the conversation.

Marketing is not one of those things that comes naturally for most people and this is a learned art just is surveillance. Being successful at both will provide a good living for a P.I. Being good at only one will make a poor P.I.

LEGALITIES OF SURVEILLANCE
Chapter Twelve

Although the author is not an attorney and does not intend to offer legal advice, there are case-laws currently on the book which investigators should be aware. These are by no means the final or sole cases related to the subject. It should be understood that the courts are constantly hearing cases that may have a bearing on the PI profession. The courts have the right to over-rule prior decisions, to restrict prior findings or to disregard prior case law all together. Those cases outlined below are cited because they have a direct bearing on the PI profession. Many cases on the books are law enforcement related and while they may have similarities, they may not actually apply due to differences in legal requirements (ex: search and seizure). Therefore please consider the following case findings with these circumstances in mind.

Any video (or other evidence) has to meet the basic elements of evidence and this is why the PI may be called upon to testify as to their findings and how they obtained the documentation. The basic prerequisites of admissibility are relevance, materiality, and competence. In general, if evidence is shown to be relevant, material, and competent, and is not barred by an exclusionary rule, it is admissible. Evid. Code § 351; Fed. Rules Evid. 402.[4]

DeLuna -v- State of Texas (1986): Part of the court's findings involved a decision that photographs are admissible as evidence if they accurately depict the subject at the time they were taken.

Darden -v- State of Texas (1982): The court ruled on several issues that included the admissibility of motion pictures and photographs as evidence. The court decided that motion pictures and photographs are admissible as evidence provided there is proof of their accuracy as correct representations of the subject at the given time and they have material relevance.

Johnson -v- State of Texas (1977): The court delivered a finding

---

[4]

http://corporate.findlaw.com/litigation-disputes/summary-of-the-rules-of-evidence.html that photographs that fairly and accurately depict the subject are generally admissible and any discrepancies between the photograph and the subject at the relevant time, if properly pointed out, will not render the photograph inadmissible.

Terry -v- State of Texas (1973): The court indicated that photographs are admissible in evidence and sighted the theory that they are pictorial communications of the witness who uses them, instead of-or in addition to, some other method of communication.

Hall -v- State of Texas (1992): The court ruled that under Rule 1001 which governs the admissions of photographs, including video tapes, the " 7 prong test " must be satisfied. The 7-prong test consists of the following:

1) It must be proved that the recording device (camera) was capable of taking testimony. Note: The investigator must be able to show that the camera was in good operating condition without malfunctions.

2) The operator of the recording device must be shown to be competent in the use and operation of the device.

3) The authenticity and correctness of the recording must be documented. Note: The investigator must be able to document the proper chain of custody and that tampering with the tape has not occurred.

4) The investigator must be able to show that the tape or photographs have not had any additions, deletions or changes made to the tape. Note: The investigator must be able to testify that the tape is a true and complete recording, free of editing or tampering of any kind. If a tape is edited, the original unedited copy must be available for review by the court.

5) The court must be shown the manner of presentation.

6) The recordings must show proper identification of the subjects depicted in the tape or photographs. Note: The investigator must have proper facial views of the subject

documented so that the identity of the subjects can be assessed.

7) Must be able to show that the testimony or actions was elicited voluntarily without inducement. Note: This goes directly to the "entrapment" of a subject. The investigator cannot cause a situation that would create circumstances that would make the subject act differently than they might without the circumstances presented to them. Example: The investigator cannot let the air out of a tire to cause the subject to have to change the tire.

U.S. -v- Pretzinger (1976): The court indicated that the attachment of an electronic location device to a vehicle moving about on public thoroughfares or through public air or public space does not infringe upon any reasonable expectation of privacy and does not constitute a search. Therefore no search warrant is needed for installation of the device. Note: The investigator should remember other laws such as trespassing laws when considering the use of these devices. If the investigator has to enter upon the property of the subject to affix the device on the vehicle, trespassing may have occurred.

U.S. -v- Mendoza (1978): The court made a ruling on the admissibility of tape recordings that were made with the consent of one party to a conversation (ex: an undercover officer). The court ruled that judicial authorization to record conversations is not necessary in these situations.

U.S. -v- Torres (1984): According to the findings in this case, television surveillance of suspected criminals and criminality is not unconstitutional.

U.S. -v- Rizzo (1978): The court found that in this case, a private investigator was attempting to gather evidence of marital infidelity on behalf of their client. The court stated that regardless of whether or not the private investigator installed an electronic device for recording conversations over the telephone or procured the client-spouse to install it by giving her the device and instructing her on how to use it, they violated the provision against interception of wire or oral communications.

White -v- Weiss (1976): The court found that when a private investigator used, or gave their client an electronic device to record telephone conversations even though it was within the client's own home and it involved one spouse against another violated the wiretap provisions of the Omnibus Crime Control and Safe Streets Act.

U.S. -v- Myers (1982): In a case in which undercover agents videotaped a conversation with a Congressman, the court ruled that the agents did not violate the Congressmen's 1st and 4th Amendment Rights.

Air Line Pilot's Association, International -v- United Airlines: The court ruled that it is a violation of the National Labor Relations Act to unlawfully photograph a picket line if it is intended to coerce or interfere.

National Labor Relations Board -v- Southern Mayland Hospital: The court ruled that it is not illegal to photograph union activities in areas restricted to the union.

<u>*Ryan –v- U.S. Air Force, et al (including Kelmar Investigations)*</u>

In this case investigators were asked to document the activities of the plaintiff who lived in a rural setting. Plaintiff sued the client, former co-workers and the PI company. The plaintiff alleged that the investigator trespassed both physically and via video. In the video the sign of a church can be seen in the video and as the video camera panned the investigators car can be seen followed by the street, barbed-wire fence and then the claimant. The investigator used a standard off-the-shelf video Sony video camera so no additional "high-tech" equipment was utilized as alleged.

1) Fifth Circuit held there is no reasonable expectation of privacy under the 4th Amendment from the use of readily available consumer-grade zoom technology
2) The court held that Ryan had neither a subjective nor an objective expectation of privacy in his activities outside his home even though his residence was bordered by several large

buildings, trees, an electric fence, and parked vehicles arranged to obstruct the view of his home.
3) Ryan tried to raise the "unlawful search and seizure" by stating the Air Force did not have the authority or properly hire Kelmar. Court dismissed this as well.

Admissibility of Digital Photographs and Video[5]

When digital imaging is considered for law enforcement, the concern of the admissibility of digital photographic evidence in court is often raised. The fact that digital photographs are more easily altered than film-based photographs is usually cited. Some even believe digital photographs are not admissible in court.

This article is presented in the hope of clearing up some of the confusion and misinformation about this issue. We will begin with the rules of evidence regarding digital evidence.

The Federal Level

Federal Rules of Evidence, Article X (Contents of Writings, Recordings and Photographs), Rule 101(1) defines writings and recordings to include magnetic, mechanical or electronic recordings.

Rule 101(3) states that if data are stored in a computer or similar device, any printout or other output readable by sight, shown to reflect the data accurately, is an "original".

Rule 101(4) states that a duplicate is a counterpart produced by the same impression as the original…by mechanical or electronic re-recording, … or by other equivalent techniques which accurately reproduces the original.

Rule 103 (Admissibility of Duplicates) states a duplicate is admissible to the same extent as an original unless (a) a genuine question is raised as to the authenticity of the original or (b) in the circumstances it would be unfair to admit the duplicate in lieu of the original. This means (1) a photograph can be stored digitally in a

---

[5] Steven B. Staggs -
http://www.crime-scene-investigator.net/admissibilityofdigital.html

computer (2) that a digital photograph stored in a computer is considered an original and (3) any exact copy of the digital photograph is admissible as evidence.

The State Level

A check your state's rules of evidence should be conducted for specifics on the admissibility of digital photographs. Most states have laws that apply to digital evidence and they usually align pretty closely to the federal rulings.

Photographs as Evidence

The principal requirements to admit a photograph (digital or film-based) into evidence are relevance and authentication. Unless the photograph is admitted by the stipulation of both parties, the party attempting to admit the photograph into evidence must be prepared to offer testimony that the photograph is an accurate representation of the scene. This usually means someone must testify that the photograph accurately portrays the scene as viewed by that witness.

Guidelines for Ensuring Your Digital Photographs Are Admissible

- Develop a Standard Operating Procedure (SOP), Department Policy, or General Order on the use of digital imaging. The SOP should include when digital imaging is used, chain of custody, image security, image enhancement, and release and availability of digital images. The SOP should not apply just to digital, but should also include film-based and video applications as well.

- Most importantly, preserve the original digital image. This can be done a variety of ways including saving the image file to a hard drive or recording the image file to a CD. Some agencies elect to use image security software.

- Digital images should be preserved in their original file formats. The saving of a file in some file formats subject the image to loss when compressed. If loss by compression is used critical image information may be lost and artifacts introduced as a result of the compression process.

- If images are stored on a computer workstation or server, and several individuals would have access to the image files, make the files read-only for all but your evidence or photo lab staff. As an example, detectives could view any image files but they would not have rights to delete or overwrite those files.

- If an image is to be analyzed or enhanced the new image files created should be saved as new file names. The original file must not be replaced (overwritten) with a new file.

Trespassing Laws

Many cases associated with violations by both PI's and law enforcement officers stem from violating trespassing laws. You cannot enter onto another person's property to place a GPS unit on a car (without written permission from the spouse/client). You also cannot trespass on someone else's property to search through their garbage. Once the garbage is placed at the street curb it is then on the city right-of-way and can legally be obtained. I always recommend that the trash be photographed at the curb to document the PI did not trespass.

Posing as a Police Officer

A PI cannot impersonate a police officer. Additionally each state may have their own regulations regarding the use of a badge. In Texas for instance, a PI can use a badge according to Administrative Licensing (Chapter 35):[6]

"No licensee shall have a badge, shield or insignia as part of any uniform, identification card or markings on a motor vehicle *containing the Flag of the State of Texas*, except those

---

[6] RULE §35.34 Standards of Conduct (b)

identification and license items that are prepared or issued by the board. No licensee shall use the Flag of the State of Texas to advertise or publicize a commercial undertaking".

Cell Phone "Pinging"

The closely watched case, in the United States Court of Appeals for the Fifth Circuit[7], is the first ruling that squarely addresses the constitutionality of warrantless searches of historical location data stored by cellphone service providers. Ruling 2 to 1, the court said a warrantless search was "not per se unconstitutional" because location data was "clearly a business record" and therefore not protected by the Fourth Amendment. Historical location data is crucial to law enforcement officials. Mr. Eckenwiler offered the example of drug investigations: A cellphone carrier can establish where a suspect met his supplier and how often he returned to a particular location. Likewise, location data can be vital in establishing people's habits and preferences, including whether they worship at a church or mosque or whether they are present at a political protest, which is why, civil liberties advocates say, it should be accorded the highest privileges of privacy protection.

Other Case Law:

Electronic Communications Privacy Act of 1986[8] (**ECPA**, codified at 18 U.S.C. §§ 2510–2522) was enacted by the United States Congress to extend government restrictions on wire taps from telephone calls to include transmissions of electronic data by computer. Specifically, ECPA was an amendment to Title III of the Omnibus Crime Control and Safe Streets Act of 1968 (the Wiretap Statute), which was primarily designed to prevent unauthorized government access to private electronic communications.

Gramm-Leach-Bliley Act[9] 15 USC, Subchapter I, Sec. 6801 -6809 - Disclosure of Nonpublic Personal Information deals with disclosing personal information.

---

[7] NY Times - www.nytimes.com/2013/07/31/technology/warrantless-cellphone-tracking
[8] http://en.wikipedia.org/wiki/Electronic_Communications_Privacy_Act
[9] http://www.ftc.gov/privacy/glbact/glbsub1.htm

<u>General Notes:</u>   It is apparent that the court has ruled that a person has the right to privacy if a reasonable and prudent person would have an expectation of privacy under similar circumstances. If a person has the garage door open and you can see the subject from the street without any binoculars or other visual assistance, the person can't expect to have a total sense of privacy. Whereas, a subject in their own home with the doors and curtains closed would be expected to have a certain degree of privacy. Common sense goes a long way in this type of work. Remember, it is your business, livelihood and reputation on the line. Making a few dollars illegally is not worth the long-term circumstances. If the situation involves trespassing, entrapment or some other violation, *think before you commit.*

SO YOU WANT TO BE A PI ?
Chapter Thirteen

According to the Bureau of Labor Statistics, in 2012 there were approximately 109,230 private investigators throughout the United States.[10] The starting average annual salary is $39,900 ($19.18 per hour) and the median salary is $74,300 ($35.72 per hour).

National estimates for this occupation:
Employment estimate and mean wage estimates for this occupation:

Employment (1)	Employment RSE (3)	Mean hourly wage	Mean annual wage (2)	Wage RSE (3)
109,230	0.5 %	$37.43	$77,860	0.4 %

Percentile wage estimates for this occupation:

Percentile	10%	25%	50% (Median)	75%	90%
Hourly Wage	$19.18	$25.16	$35.72	$47.57	$59.13
Annual Wage (2)	$39,900	$52,320	$74,300	$98,940	$122,990

However, these statistics from the Bureau of Labor Statistics is high suspect as it does not speak directly to *private investigators* as a standalone profession. Their statistics (see below) deal with those listed as an investigator in university, hospitals, government and related jobs and are therefore not truly private investigators. A true private investigator does not work for a single employer. According to definition, a private investigator "is a person who can be hired by individuals or groups to undertake investigatory law services".[11]

---

[10] http://www.bls.gov/oes/current/oes333021.htm
[11] http://en.wikipedia.org/wiki/Private_investigator

Industries with the highest levels of employment in this occupation:

Industry	Employment (1)	Percent of industry employment	Hourly mean wage	Annual mean wage (2)
Local Government (OES Designation)	46,250	0.85	$31.06	$64,610
Federal Executive Branch (OES Designation)	43,450	2.13	$48.22	$100,290
State Government (OES Designation)	18,820	0.86	$28.11	$58,460
Postal Service	520	0.08	$43.07	$89,580
Colleges, Universities, and Professional Schools	100	0.00	$32.35	$67,280

Industries with the highest concentration of employment in this occupation:

Industry	Employment (1)	Percent of industry employment	Hourly mean wage	Annual mean wage (2)
Federal Executive Branch (OES Designation)	43,450	2.13	$48.22	$100,290
State Government (OES Designation)	18,820	0.86	$28.11	$58,460
Local Government (OES Designation)	46,250	0.85	$31.06	$64,610
Postal Service	520	0.08	$43.07	$89,580
Psychiatric and Substance Abuse Hospitals	60	0.02	$32.29	$67,160

Top paying industries for this occupation:

Industry	Employment (1)	Percent of industry employment	Hourly mean wage	Annual mean wage (2)
Federal Executive Branch (OES Designation)	43,450	2.13	$48.22	$100,290
Postal Service	520	0.08	$43.07	$89,580
Colleges, Universities, and Professional Schools	100	(7)	$32.35	$67,280
Psychiatric and Substance Abuse Hospitals	60	0.02	$32.29	$67,160
Local Government (OES Designation)	46,250	0.85	$31.06	$64,610

To be more industry specific, information from the Texas Association of Licensed Investigators [12] revealed the following statistics based on a 2011 survey of membership:

*Statistics based on the number of association members responding to survey.

What is your current age:

21-25	1.00%
26-30	1.75%
31-35	6.50%
36-40	8.25%
41-45	12.75%
46-50	17.25%
51-55	29.50%
56-60	13.25%
61-65	6.50%
66-70	3.25%
71-+	0.00%

---

[12] TALI – www.TALI.org

What is your *company's* gross income:

LESS THAN $50,000	28.57%
$50,000-75,000	3.57%
$75,100-100,000	14.29%
$100,1100-125,000	10.71%
$125,100-150,000	0.00%
$150,100-175,000	7.14%
$175,100-200.000	3.57%
200,100-250,000	3.57%
250,100-300,000	0.00%
300,100-350,000	10.71%
350,100-400,000	0.00%
400,100-500,000	0.00%
500,100-750,000	3.57%
750,100-1,000,000	7.14%
1,000,100-2,000,000	3.57%
2,000,000-3,000,000	0.00%
3,000,000-5,000,000	3.57%

How many investigators work for your agency or the agency you are employed by:

1	48.15%
2	18.52%
3	11.11%
4	0.00%
5	7.41%
6	0.00%
7	0.00%

8	3.70%
9	0.00%
10 to 15	7.41%
16 to 20	0.00%
21 to 25	3.70%
26 or more	1.00%

What is the primary source of your income (case types):

Criminal Defense	8.63%
Personal Injury	7.91%
Domestic Matters (fidelity, custody, divorce, etc)	9.35%
Criminal Prosecution	2.88%
Pre-employment	5.76%
Backgrounds	11.51%
Civil Cases	12.23%
Insurance Cases	9.35%
White Collar	4.32%
Adoptions	2.16%
Missing persons	3.60%
Interviews (witnesses, claimants, applicants, etc)	10.79%
Personal Protection (Bodyguard)	2.16%
Security	2.88%
Technical Countermeasures	1.44%
Mystery Shopping services	0.00%
I do whatever walks in the door	3.60%
Mitigation issues	1.44%
I sale only and sub contract out the work	0.00%
I do only the items checked above	0.00%

How did you gain your experience:

Insurance industry investigations	7.32%
Prior local or state Law Enforcement experience	26.83%
Prior Legal related employment	7.32%
Banking, collections, lending experience	0.00%
Military experience	4.88%
Registered PI for another licensee	21.95%
Federal Law enforcement	14.63%
Federal Intelligence Agency experience	4.88%
Business experience	2.44%
Undercover experience	2.44%
Sales Experience	2.44%
Security primarily with some investigation	0.00%
Self-employed and got credit for my work	0.00%
Something else entirely	4.88%

How long have you been employed as a PI:

Less than 2 years	6.25%
2-5 Years	31.25%
6-10 Years	15.62%
11-15 Years	18.75%
16+ Years	28.12%

When you work as a PI it is:

My Only Job?	48.48%
My Post Retirement Job?	24.24%
My Part-time job?	6.06%
One of several businesses?	21.21%
Something to stay busy?	0.00%

This sheds some closer light on the job functions and performance of those actually involved in the profession and not subject to a random government poll of the non-PI related jobs.

TALI Summary

The summary of the Texas Association of Licensed Investigators poll indicates:

1) the average age of private investigators are middle-aged (41-60)

2) almost half of all PI agencies are 1 person operations (48.15%);

3) slightly more than 33% get their income from backgrounds and civil cases

A closer look finds the following statistics more closely in line with the actual field. According this information, a private investigator makes $36,000 to $86,000.[13]

---

[13] http://www.indeed.com/salary/Investigator.html

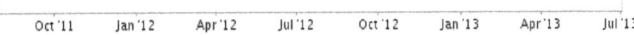

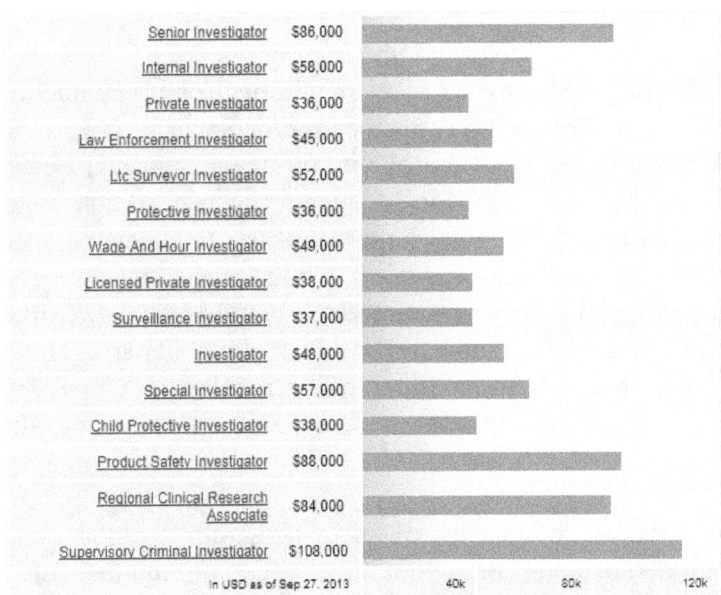

In a survey conducted by the PI Magazine, the survey results found that less than 16% of all male PIs are younger than 41. The majority group seems to be those male private investigators in the 41 - 50 year old bracket at 31%. However, the current survey results revealed that 52% of all male PI's are over 50 years of age, of which 22% are over 60. The PI Magazine also concluded the size of agencies as reported by PI's:

1 Person – 66%
2 People – 11% (owner plus one full-time employee)
3-5 Employees (full-time) 18%
6-10 Employees (full-time) 2%
11+ Employees (full-time) 3%

To want to become a PI isn't an original idea and based on the above statistics, you are going to have to be exceptionally good at your job to stick out of the crowd. Even if you are the best thing going, it doesn't matter unless you can market your services and get the cases in to begin with. Once you have the assignment, then it is up to you to dazzle them and provide a work product, written report, video and supporting documents that will reassure the client that they selected the right PI for the job.

But how does a person go about getting started? To become a licensed private investigator, you should begin with contacting the State Board of Private Investigators and/or Security Guards that is usually located in the Capitol city in your State. Request an application for a PI and for an agency license. Each state has different requirements with some requiring no licensing, several years of education and experience and everything in between. Besides the qualification requirements, you also have to find out what your State's insurance and bond requirements are. However, most states are set up in the same general way with only the education, experience and insurance requirements being slightly different.

For instance, to own a private investigation agency, you will have to demonstrate that you have a certain number of years experience as a police officer or private investigator. There will probably be an education requirement (high school or college) and a test covering the state's PI requirements that will have to be passed. Once the requirements to own an agency are met, you will then have to prove that you have liability insurance, have filed corporate documents with the State Comptroller's office and/or Secretary of State's office, provide proof that you are bonded (where applicable), and possibly meet other requirements.

It is also important to note that it is a criminal and/or civil offense to operate as a PI without properly being licensed. In the State of Texas as an example, private investigators are subject to the Texas Occupations Code 1702 and Chapter 35 Administrative Rules.

§1702.101. INVESTIGATIONS COMPANY LICENSE REQUIRED.
Unless the person holds a license as an investigations company, a person may not:
(1) act as an investigations company;
(2) offer to perform the services of an investigations company; or

(3) engage in business activity for which a license is required under this chapter.

§1702.103. CLASSIFICATION AND LIMITATION OF LICENSES.

(a) The license classifications are:
(1) Class A: investigations company license, covering operations of an investigations company;
(2) Class B: security services contractor license, covering operations of a security services contractor;
(3) Class C: covering the operations included within Class A and Class B; and
(4) Class D: electronic access control device license, covering operations of an electronic access control device company.
(b) A Class A, B, C, or D license does not authorize the license holder to perform a service for which the license holder has not qualified. A person may not engage in an operation outside the scope of that person's license. The commission shall indicate on the license the services the license holder is authorized to perform. The license holder may not perform a service unless it is indicated on the license.

§1702.104. INVESTIGATIONS COMPANY.

(a) A person acts as an investigations company for the purposes of this chapter if the person:
(1) engages in the business of obtaining or furnishing, or accepts employment to obtain or furnish, information related to:
(A) crime or wrongs done or threatened against a state or the United States;
(B) the identity, habits, business, occupation, knowledge, efficiency, loyalty, movement, location, affiliations, associations, transactions, acts, reputation, or character of a person;
(C) the location, disposition, or recovery of lost or stolen property; or
(D) the cause or responsibility for a fire, libel, loss, accident, damage, or injury to a person or to property;

CHAPTER 1702, OCCUPATIONS CODE §1702.112. 7

(2) engages in the business of securing, or accepts employment to secure, evidence for use before a court, board, officer, or investigating committee;

(3) engages in the business of securing, or accepts employment to secure, the electronic tracking of the location of an individual or motor vehicle other than for criminal justice purposes by or on behalf of a governmental entity; or

(4) engages in the business of protecting, or accepts employment to protect, an individual from bodily harm through the use of a personal protection officer.

(b) For purposes of Subsection (a)(1), obtaining or furnishing information includes information obtained or furnished through the review and analysis of, and the investigation into the content of, computer-based data not available to the public.

In Florida, you will see that the definitions and requirements are very similar. In Florida private investigators are regulated by Chapter 493 of the Private Investigation Statutes:

(15) "Private investigative agency" means any person who, for consideration, advertises as providing or is engaged in the business of furnishing private investigations.

(16) "Private investigator" means any individual who, for consideration, advertises as providing or performs private investigation. This does not include an informant who, on a one-time or limited basis, as a result of a unique expertise, ability, vocation, or special access and who, under the direction and control of a Class "C" licensee or a Class "MA" licensee, provides information or services that would otherwise be included in the definition of private investigation.

(17) "Private investigation" means the investigation by a person or persons for the purpose of obtaining information with reference to any of the following matters:

(a) Crime or wrongs done or threatened against the United States or any state or territory of the United States, when operating under express written authority of the governmental official responsible for authorizing such investigation.

(b) The identity, habits, conduct, movements, whereabouts, affiliations, associations, transactions, reputation, or character of any society, person, or group of persons.

(c) The credibility of witnesses or other persons.

(d) The whereabouts of missing persons, owners of unclaimed property or escheated property, or heirs to estates.

(e) The location or recovery of lost or stolen property.

(f) The causes and origin of, or responsibility for, fires, libels, slanders, losses, accidents, damage, or injuries to real or personal property.

(g) The business of securing evidence to be used before investigating committees or boards of award or arbitration or in the trial of civil or criminal cases and the preparation therefor.

493.6106 License requirements; posting.--

(1) Each individual licensed by the department must:

(a) Be at least 18 years of age.

(b) Be of good moral character.

(c) Not have been adjudicated incapacitated under s. 744.331 or a similar statute in another state, unless her or his capacity has been judicially restored; not have been involuntarily placed in a treatment facility for the mentally ill under chapter 394 or a similar statute in any other state, unless her or his competency has been judicially restored; and not have been diagnosed as having an incapacitating mental illness, unless a psychologist or psychiatrist licensed in this state certifies that she or he does not currently suffer from the mental illness.

(d) Not be a chronic and habitual user of alcoholic beverages to the extent that her or his normal faculties are impaired; not have been committed under chapter 397, former chapter 396, or a similar law in any other state; not have been found to be a habitual offender under s. 856.011(3) or a similar law in any other state; and not have had two or more convictions under s. 316.193 or a similar law in any other state within the 3-year period immediately preceding the date the application was filed, unless the individual establishes that she or he is not currently impaired and has successfully completed a rehabilitation course.

(e) Not have been committed for controlled substance abuse or have been found guilty of a crime under chapter 893 or a similar law relating to controlled substances in any other state within a 3-year period immediately preceding the date the application was filed, unless the individual establishes that she or he is not currently abusing any controlled substance and has successfully completed a rehabilitation course.

(f) Be a citizen or legal resident alien of the United States or have been granted authorization to seek employment in this country by the United States Bureau of Citizenship and Immigration Services.

(2) Each agency shall have a minimum of one physical location within this state from which the normal business of the agency is conducted, and this location shall be considered the primary office for that agency in this state.

(a) If an agency desires to change the physical location of the business, as it appears on the agency license, the department must be notified within 10 days of the change, and, except upon renewal, the fee prescribed in s. 493.6107 must be submitted for each license requiring revision. Each license requiring revision must be returned with such notification.

(b) The Class "A," Class "B," or Class "R" license and any branch office or school license shall at all times be posted in a conspicuous place at the licensed physical location in this state where the business is conducted.

(c) Each Class "A," Class "B," Class "R," branch office, or school licensee shall display, in a place that is in clear and unobstructed public view, a notice on a form prescribed by the department stating that the business operating at this location is licensed and regulated by the Department of Agriculture and Consumer Services and that any questions or complaints should be directed to the department.

(d) A minimum of one properly licensed manager shall be designated for each agency and branch office location.

You will see therefore that most state licensing requirements are very similar. In the State of Texas, you are required to have a minimum of 3 years of experience to own or manage an agency. The University of North Texas/Professional Development Institute is currently the only academic curriculum that you can take that will qualify you to sit for the manager's test.

If you do not qualify to own and/or manage a private investigation company, you will then have to consider being employed through a private investigation company so that you can gain the necessary experience that will allow you to open your own agency. Sometimes, PI agencies will hire college students on a training basis. You may even have to donate some of your time to an agency to get your foot in the door. Just because you do not have any direct experience as a police officer or PI doesn't mean you may not qualify. If you were an insurance adjuster, paralegal, reporter or worked in some other field where you can demonstrate that you were involved in research and/or investigations, you still may be able to meet the requirements.

Also, to gain some credentials in the PI field, I would recommend that you find out where seminars, conventions and classes associated with the PI field are being held and attend. First, you will gain valuable experience through those who have already demonstrated a proficiency in the field. In addition, you will have the opportunity to meet and become acquainted with PI's that may provide a source of employment or future case assignments. Some of the organizations that you can get in touch with to find out about seminars and conventions are:

N.A.I.S.: National Association of Investigative Specialists, based in Austin, Texas Telephone #: (512) 719-3595

A.S.I.S.: American Society of Industrial Specialists (703) 522-5800

T.A.L.I.: Texas Association of Licensed Investigators

N.A.L.I.: National Association of Licensed Investigators

P.I. Mall: Located on the Internet

State Board of PI's located in your particular State, as well as the State Association of PI's in your State.

If, in fact, you discover that you do not meet the requirements to become a PI and/or owner of your own agency and find that you have been unsuccessful in getting hired by an agency, you may wish to consider other related jobs that may or may not come under the control of the State Board of Private Investigators. Some of these include:

Bounty Hunter: The individual who tracks down, apprehends and returns a subject to the court that holds a warrant for their arrest in return for monetary remuneration.

Bail Bondsman: The person responsible for placing a bond for the release of a person from jail for a percentage of the total bond amount.

Information Broker: The person who provides information for PI's, attorneys, insurance adjusters and private industry. This can include database searches or simply retrieving copies of records from courthouse records.

Missing Heir Locator: A person who checks the probate records and locates missing heirs of an estate in exchange for a portion of the recovered proceeds.

Child Support Mediator: A person who locates a spouse who owes back child support in exchange for a set fee or portion of the recovered proceeds.

Child Recovery Expert: A person who tracks down and locates missing children.

Adoption Locator: A person who attempts to locate unknown

siblings, biological parents or relatives.

Note: It should be understood that some or all of these jobs may still come under the supervision of the State Board of PI's in your particular State and should be fully investigated before proceeding into these areas.

Disclaimer: Kelmar and Associates, Inc., and/or Kelly E. Riddle individually provides the information enclosed in "The Art of Surveillance" strictly for the use of licensed private investigators and law enforcement officers working in the scope of their employment and is not intended for the use of the average, non-trained person.

COUNTER SURVEILLANCE
Chapter Fourteen

In this business, we are often called upon to wear several different hats. This is true with surveillance as well. You should not always assume that you and your client are the only ones watching another party. You and/or your client may be the victim of surveillance.

Often times, we are called to conduct counter surveillance for clients that are being accused of harassing someone or of being in a certain location when they are not actually there. We have been asked to conduct counter surveillance during child custody situations. However, when you think of "counter surveillance," you typically think of one spy watching another. This is usually on the government level, although corporate spies often watch each other.

One of the more common types of counter surveillance is related to executives to insure they are not being followed or set up for kidnapping. Like any other type of case, an investigator should first evaluate the reason for the counter surveillance. In other words, "why does the client believe they are a target of a threat?" The next question is, "will the threat come from professionals and how sophisticated are the attackers?"

Types of Threats: For the most part, potential threats come from the following general categories:

1) Sexual Deviant/Child Molester

2) Extortionist
    a) Money
    b) Information/trade secrets

3) Terrorist
    a) Political statement
    b) Damage reputation
    c) Vengeance

4) Domestic/Child Custody

The sexual deviant consists of various levels of threat. The first is a simple need to be around the person they are infatuated with to enable their inappropriate feelings to gain justification. If they can get near a movie star, they receive some gratification while being able to justify the lack of direct attention due to the star having to "work," or the star ignoring them to prevent the press from catching on to their "relationship." Unfortunately, this person usually starts by simply requesting a photograph of the star. When received, they magnify that into a form of confirmation of the star's love for them. Eventually, the person needs more attention and may send letters, stalk, conduct their own surveillance and finally attack the person. Examples of this include John Lennon, and Giovanni Versace.

The extortionist conducts surveillance to determine how easy it will be to kidnap the target. While watching the person, the kidnapper will also seek to evaluate the target's routine activities. This allows the kidnapper to plan their attack more precisely based on known factors. The famous case of Charles Lindburgh is an example of this type of counter surveillance. A more common example of extortion involves information and trade secrets prevalent in cold war espionage.

The terrorist conducts counter surveillance to determine the weaknesses of the target. The United States Embassy in Africa, the Government Building in Oklahoma City and the 9-1-1 attacks are prominent examples of these cases. Just as important of examples are the bombings in the Middle East. These are done to make a political statement, damage the reputation of the U.S. and their allies and to extract vengeance.

We have been on surveillance and found that other investigators from another company are on the same case. The client may have forgotten whom they assigned the case to, or they may be checking to see if the two companies are consistent with the other investigators. All the more reason why you should keep an eye out for others around you while doing surveillance, to insure you and your client are not the target or surveillance.

<u>Executive Counter Surveillance:</u> Our company was asked to

watch the President of a computer related business while the executive was in town on business. The President had received threatening letters from a former employee. The idea was to keep the executive and the former employee under surveillance until the President left town. Our investigators performed some pre-surveillance intelligence by observing the former employee for a day to get a better idea of their activities and driving habits. Throughout the following three days, each team of investigators would communicate if the former employee left their residence. Fortunately, a threat was never realized. However, keeping an executive under surveillance to prevent surveillance without letting them become aware of the surveillance isn't as easy as it seems. The executive changed their schedule numerous times, causing complications. It is very similar to the President of the United States deciding to step out of his vehicle to shake hands when that was not a scheduled event. The Secret Service Agents have to scramble to secure the President without it being obvious.

The key goals of counter surveillance include:

1) identify and analysis of threats

2) prevention of the avoidable

3) detection of the avoidable

4) response to crisis

The first goal should be to analyze the potential threat and identify those responsible for the threat. This could be a single individual, group or terrorist cell. When a bombing or other unusual crisis occurs, the first job is to identify who is responsible. Often times, many groups will claim responsibility when in fact, they are not the responsible parties.

According to the National Institute of Justice, there are more than 1.4 million victims of stalking each year. The majority of victims have had some type of business or personal relationship with their stalkers.

Prevention of the avoidable deals primarily with physical security and procedures that can be evaluated and changed prior to a threat. It is better to be proactive instead of reacting after the fact.

Detection of the avoidable includes using technology and monitoring of the potential target. This can be done through the use of GPS tracking devices, CCTV cameras, infrared photo-electric beams and related equipment. Through the use of these devices, you should be notified of a breach of security in time to react.

Once a threat is initiated, the response to the crisis will depend a great deal on the outcome. A plan of action should be in place to identify a course of action, who should be notified, and what specific plans should be executed. As an example, in the event that a threat against a C.E.O. is obtained, an immediate increase in perimeter security should result. The executive's location should be determined and changed to a secured and pre-designated area. Communication with other key executives should entail, as well as law enforcement. A plan of action, including a decision of whether to move the executive, what routes and what methods should be enacted.

Remember that in extortion and most personal threat situations, the attackers want to capture and not kill. Money is the issue, and they may need the victim to prove they are alive. The attack must take place within a two-minute time frame to be effective. In addition, the attack is a result of security breeches or failed procedures.

The majority of attacks and kidnapping take place either at the residence or out on the roadway. The residence should be secured with the use of technology. Failure to activate or utilize this technology usually results in the necessary breech needed by the attacker.

Vehicle attacks are based on common, routine routes where a particular location of attack and surprise can be carried out effectively. Using construction and natural terrain assists in the surprise and attack.

Using Traffic Lanes for Defense/Protection

___

   ___   ___   ___

   ___   ___   ___

   ___   ___   ___

___

Recognize the lane you choose makes a difference

In the preceding diagram, using the middle lane gives your attacker the opportunity to box you in. However, the outside lane may not be any better if there is not a shoulder, grass or some other avenue of escape. The following diagram is an example of using the middle lane inappropriately.

The Block or "Squeeze" Technique

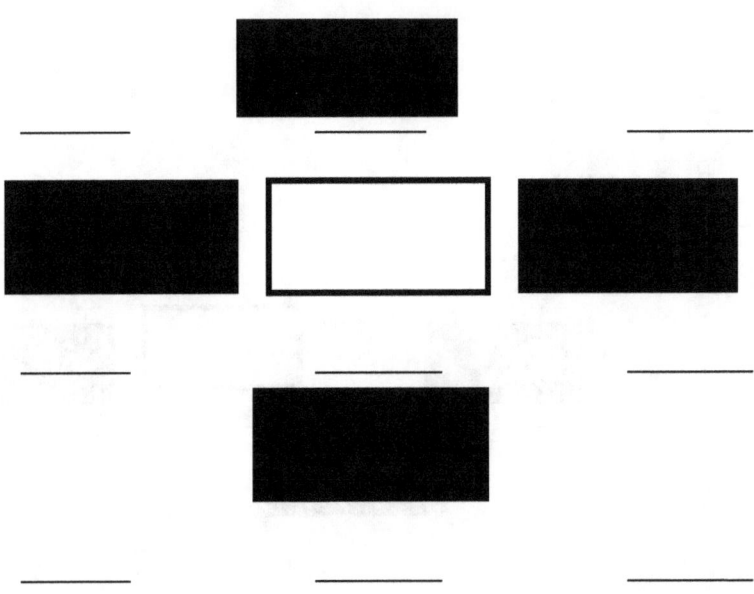

To Avoid: Stay in Outside Lanes (2) Maintain distance between vehicles (3) Observation

In the event of an ambush, you should be capable of evasive maneuvers. An example is as follows:

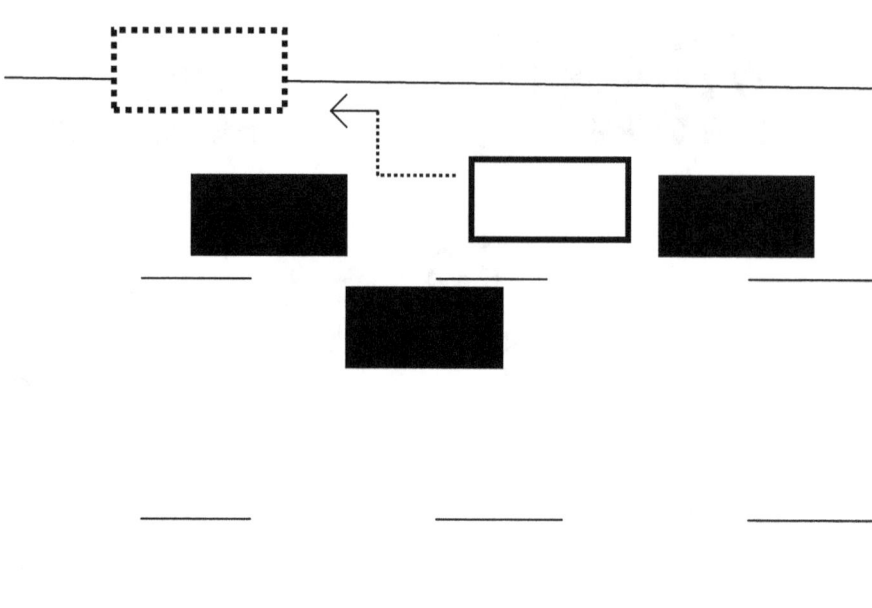

Avoiding the "Squeeze" (Proper Lane Use)

To Avoid: Maintain Proper Distance (2) Respond Immediately (3) Maneuver around block vehicles quickly (4) Do Not Stop for any reason (5) Proceed to Alternate Route (6) Continue to Safe House

Some of the more common mistakes when involved in counter surveillance in vehicles include:

1) Panic: Due to a failure to properly train and prepare. A good investigator will use adrenalin to their advantage.

2) Using Vehicle to Ram: May cause injury and crippling damage to your own vehicle. Proper identification of the impending attack and training to avoid these circumstances can prevent this from the onset.

3) Failure to Adhere to Alternative Routes: In the event of a crisis, pre-arranged alternative routes should be taken. Failure to abide by these safeguards may lead you into additional trouble.

4) Knowing whether to proceed forward or back: This can be a life or death decision as you know what is behind you but not what is ahead.

HEAD - ON "INTERCEPTION" WITH SUPPORT

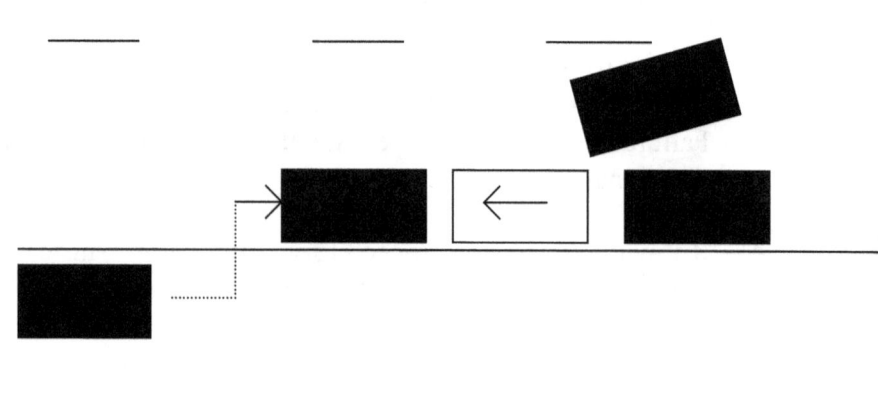

To Avoid: Stay in Outside Lanes (2) Maintain distance between vehicles (3) **Observation**

The preceding diagram shows how easy it is to become a sandwich with vehicles coming from you from both directions. To properly avoid counter surveillance and kidnap attempts, aggressive proactive measures need to be in place. This includes constant evaluation of the street, vehicles, traffic, police and related activity.

Like any other skill, this is one that requires the investigator to constantly train and evolve. Knowing your enemy is a good start. Information gathering, good intelligence information and proper training will provide for successful counter surveillance.

GPS TRACKING DEVICES & DRONES
Chapter Fifteen

The use of satellites and GPS (global positioning system) tracking devices is increasing for various reasons and are getting more and more common. As this progresses and the costs come down, the PI industry will benefit from this technology. There are numerous applications for using this technology including tracking stolen equipment, locating missing children or elderly parents, tracking suspected infidelity partners and similar situations we may be called upon to provide solutions for our clients and customers. Using satellite and cell tracking technology are sources of remedying a situation for our clients.

The most common type of GPS tracking is through cell phone tower triangulation. The majority of public sector units operate by locating the signal within three different cell phone towers. The user will be given the latitude and longitude coordinates and/or a physical address. This is not pin-point accurate information but gets the user in the general location of the GPS signal. For instance, if the information indicates the unit is at 589 Main Street, it may actually be at a different address further down on the same street. If there is an intersection nearby, the signal may actually be just around the corner on the cross-street. Understanding that GPS signals are not absolutely accurate is extremely important in an investigation. With this understanding the PI should not rely solely on the GPS unit and should be used only in conjunction with actual physical surveillance. Additionally, tracking through GPS only tells you where the GPS unit is and not where the person is located. They could park their car and get in another vehicle. Failure to physically observe this would result in an incomplete investigation.

Other factors can affect the GPS signal including parking garages, rural areas and weather. Any location where a regular cell phone would have limited or no signal would also cause the GPS signal to respond in a similar manner.

There are two common methods for attaching a GPS unit to a vehicle. Depending on the nature of the investigation, you may be limited to only accessing the exterior of the vehicle. In these situations a weatherproof box is utilized that has magnets for attaching to the undercarriage of the vehicle. The GPS is turned on, placed in the weatherproof box and attached to the vehicle.

The other method of attaching a GPS unit to a vehicle is through a "hard-wire" of the unit. There are wiring harnesses that most manufacturers of GPS units sell that allows you to simply plug the harness into the fuse box or similar wiring connector under the dash of the vehicle. In some high-dollar vehicles, an improper installation can short out electronics due to on-board computer systems. Caution should be taken in these types of installations.

There are several pros and cons of hard-wire GPS units verses magnetic weatherproof boxes on the exterior of the vehicle. The most obvious is battery life. A hard-wired unit is connected to the vehicle's battery and therefore always has a power source. The one used on the outside of the car has to depend solely on the battery life of the GPS unit. Larger battery packs can be purchased that extend the tracking time but eventually the unit has to be removed and the batter recharged. The battery life of the battery that comes with the GPS unit will normally last from 2 to 7 days. The longer extended life battery will normally give the unit 7 to 21 days. The battery life is decreased based on the amount of driving the person does as well as how many times the unit is "pinged" or asked for its location. The GPS unit can be programmed to give you the location only when it moves, every hour, every 5-10 minutes or constantly. The more it provides the location the more the battery is drained.

When looking at companies that sell GPS units, you should make sure that they have a dedicated website that you can log into and have direct access to the information. Many of these companies also have cell phone applications available. The website should be able to give you location, speed, direction of travel, battery level and report download capabilities as a minimum. Several show green arrows while traveling and red indicating they have stopped. Good sites should also allow you to set up "geo fences" that alerts you by text or email if the vehicle "breaks" or leaves that pre-set location.

From a strictly operational standpoint, the PI should consider having someone in the office that is not driving to monitor the GPS and provide details to the field investigator so they can concentrate on traffic and the actual surveillance. At night, the glare of a laptop of cell phone may also be an issue during surveillance. In a mobile situation, the use of a GPS unit gives you extra security in the event the subject is lost and allows the PI to keep more distance between the target vehicle.

Once the investigation is complete, it is recommended that you do not give a printout of the GPS log to the client. The majority of people do not understand the reports or how a GPS unit works so this may confuse and therefore bring your entire investigation into undue suspicion.

Legal Issues

The legal use of GPS tracking varies from state to state and there have been attempts on the federal level to regulate these devices as well. While the author is not an attorney and does not intend to offer legal advice herein, the topic warrants discussion.

In some jurisdictions such as Texas, there is a built in defense in criminal cases as outlined below:

Section 16.06 of the Texas Penal Code, Criminal and Traffic Law includes:

Sec. 16.06. Unlawful Installation of Tracking Device.

a) In this section:

(1) "Electronic or mechanical tracking device" means a device capable of emitting an electronic frequency or other signal that may be used by a person to identify, monitor, or record the location of another person or object.

(2) "Motor vehicle" has the meaning assigned by Section 501.002, Transportation Code.

b) A person commits an offense if the person knowingly installs an electronic or mechanical tracking device on a motor vehicle owned or leased by another person.

c) An offense under this section is a Class A misdemeanor.

d) **It is an affirmative defense to prosecution under this section that the person**:

(1) Obtained the effective consent of the owner or lessee of the motor vehicle before the electronic or mechanical tracking device was installed;

(2) Was a peace officer who installed the device in the course of a criminal investigation or pursuant to an order of a court to gather information for a law enforcement agency; or

(3) **Was a private investigator licensed under Chapter 1702, Occupations Code, who installed the device:**

(A) **With written consent:**

(i) To install the device given by the owner or lessee of the motor vehicles; and

(ii) To enter private residential property, if that entry was necessary to install the device, given by the owner or lessee of the property; or

(B) Pursuant to an order of or other authorization from a court to gather information.

Although this is a defense built into the criminal statute in Texas that certainly does not mean that a civil lawsuit cannot be brought against anyone perceived as being a violator.

You then have to take this a step further and identify who, even within a marriage, has the legal authority to authorize the installation of a GPS device on a vehicle. Some states are "community property" states and some are not. For simplification and without going into the deviations or extenuating circumstances, in a community property state any assets obtained during the marriage are considered to be equally owned by the marriage partners. Following that train of thought, if a person is concerned about infidelity and suspects their spouse of having an affair, the client/spouse may have the legal right to authorize the installation of a GPS device since they own at least half of the vehicle.

Any PI using a GPS in the course of their business should have a GPS authorization, hold harmless and release of liability contract that the client should sign before installing a GPS device. As a side note, occasionally a GPS unit will fall or get knocked off of the vehicle. The PI should therefore also include a reimbursement clause in their contract.

Texas Family Code

CHAPTER 3. MARITAL PROPERTY RIGHTS AND LIABILITIES

SUBCHAPTER A. GENERAL RULES FOR SEPARATE AND COMMUNITY PROPERTY

§ 3.001. SEPARATE PROPERTY. *A spouse's separate property consists of:*

(1) the property owned or claimed by the spouse before marriage;

(2) the property acquired by the spouse during marriage by gift, devise, or descent; and

(3) the recovery for personal injuries sustained by the spouse during marriage, except any recovery for loss of earning capacity during marriage.

Added by Acts 1997, 75th Leg., ch. 7, § 1, eff. April 17, 1997.

According to Texas law, community property is defined:

§ 3.002. COMMUNITY PROPERTY. Community property consists of the property, other than separate property, acquired by either spouse during marriage.

Added by Acts 1997, 75th Leg., ch. 7, § 1, eff. April 17, 1997.

In states where community property is not recognized, the person's name must be on the title of the car before they can grant you authority to install a GPS unit. Even in community property states it is recommended that their name be on the title as well.

Currently case law on this subject is somewhat limited to date. The bulk of the case law deals with law enforcement and the issue of a search warrant before a unit can be installed on a vehicle. One such case is:

United States v. Jones, [14]565 US ___, 132 S.Ct. 945 (2012), was a United States Supreme Court case in which the Court held that installing a Global Positioning System (GPS) tracking device on a vehicle and using the device to monitor the vehicle's movements constitutes a search under the Fourth Amendment.

In 2005 defendant Antoine Jones was suspected of drug trafficking. Police investigators asked for and received a warrant to attach a GPS tracking device to the underside of the defendant's car but then exceeded the warrant's scope in both geography and length of time. The Supreme Court justices voted unanimously that this violated the Fourth Amendment, though they were split on the reasoning. The majority held that by installing the GPS device on the defendants car the police had committed a trespass on private property and that the trespass constituted a *per se* breach of the defendant's privacy.

Author's Opinion:

There is a distinction between law enforcement and the private investigator in numerous areas with evidentiary requirements being one of these. As an example, if a law enforcement officer is going to interview someone that is or could be a suspect in a crime they have to give them their Miranda Warning[15]. A private investigator on the other hand can interview a person, get a confession from them and not be subject to the same requirements of law. The legal system puts more requirements on government officials to insure compliance to the Constitution. The public expects this and case law has supported stricter guidelines for law enforcement.

In the case of police installing a GPS unit, they are looking at gathering information to assist in filing criminal charges and the successful prosecution of the person. Even if they had the cooperation of a spouse who legal could provide them with authorization to install a GPS unit, police would still be required to

---

[14] http://en.wikipedia.org/wiki/United_States_v._Antoine_Jones
[15] http://en.wikipedia.org/wiki/Miranda_warning

obtain a search warrant. On the other hand, since the private investigator is not operating as a law enforcement official they do not have to adhere to this requirement although they still have to have legal authorization from the owner and/or spouse.

Where many PI's *could* get into a legal issue is similar to the police officers in U.S. –v- Jones where trespass was asserted. This can be an electronic trespass or a physical trespass but for most PI's the first issue would be the physical trespass. Of course, if your client gave you permission to install the GPS unit then they would have given you permission to enter their property to install the GPS unit but this should also be spelled out in any contract and authorization.

Cell Phone Tracking

In addition to regular GPS unit tracking, cell phone positioning has become a prevalent feature on most cell phones. Putting a program on someone else's telephone to record their conversations or activity is illegal under U.S. Code 18 Part 1 -Chapter 119-Wire and Electronic Communications Interception[16]. Law enforcement officers have to obtain a search warrant to obtain information related to cell phone records. However, the current argument for both law enforcement and the private sector is that "pinging" a cell phone does not extract, copy or otherwise obtain any information or data from the phone. A cell phone ping is similar to GPS unit positioning as the cell phone towers are triangulated to provide the approximate location of the phone. As with traditional GPS units, they may be mobile and therefore the location may continue to change.

Drones

The use of Unmanned Aircraft Systems (UAS), commonly referred to as "drones" has a tremendous potential for private investigators. At the moment, this is a fairly unregulated body. This will soon change and definitions will be given to categorize public

---

[16] http://www.law.cornell.edu/uscode/text/18/part-I/chapter-119

(government), private and commercial use. The Federal Aeronautics Administration (FAA) is the governing body that administrates the utilization of the National Airspace System.

At the present time FAA does not address the size of the model aircraft. The drones being used by the military range from very large to extremely small and the general public has access to a wide variety as well. The FAA stipulates that model aircraft should stay below 400 feet above ground.

Pricing varies from around $250 to almost $10,000 and the shapes vary just as widely. There are typical airplane shapes, helicopter, balloon (Hindenburg type), gyro-bladed and many others. Currently drones on the market have thermal infrared video capabilities with onboard digital video recorder (DVR), low light video, GPS coordinated routing and mapping, maneuvering via hand-held controls or smart phone applications, gyro-stabilized cameras and other features.

Thus far, some of the biggest issues with the public use of drones have been documented cases of the drone plowing into a crowd at a sporting event[17] or a wedding photographer having a drone crash into the groom during the ceremony[18]. It appears that many of these types of events take place when the battery level is depleted. Another issue is the lack of training and skill of the handler.

Legislation

According to the Electronic Frontier Foundation in an article published June 3, 2013[19], "All but seven states have proposed or adopted legislation relating to the domestic use of drones, or unmanned aerial systems, in domestic airspace, according to the

---

[17] http://www.huffingtonpost.com/2012/12/07/drone-crash-uc-san-diego_n_2258323.html

[18] http://betabeat.com/2013/08/renegade-drone-crashes-into-grooms-head-before-wedding/

[19] https://www.eff.org/deeplinks/2013/06/all-drone-legislation-must-meet-these-three-requirements

National Conference of State Legislatures. Now, at the invitation of the Aerospace States Association, EFF has rung in with the three crucial elements that all drone legislation must contain to balance privacy rights with free-speech concerns".

The proponents indicate that " **First**, law enforcement must be required to obtain warrants before using drones in investigations to protect the Fourth Amendment rights of citizens from overbroad or undue data collection. **Second**, commercial drone operators must be held to established privacy standards and must disclose the details of their operations. **Third**, legislation that regulates private and media use of drones must strike an appropriate balance between privacy and First Amendment protected activities such as newsgathering".

The National Council of Investigative and Security Services[20] that oversees legislation effecting the private investigation profession notified members that several bills had been introduced in the 2013 legislative season that attempted to regulate drones. Accordingly NCISS indicated, "Currently, non-governmental drone use is approved by the Federal Aviation Administration in a limited fashion on an experimental basis. But an expansion of the approvals is expected. In addition, the General Accountability Office testified that no federal prohibition exists for the use of model aircraft".

NCISS stated further, "Congress is becoming interested in how drones might be used within the United States by both government and private entities. Drone technology now exists so that its small size and affordability is a threat to individual privacy. Last week, the Subcommittee on Oversight, Investigations, and Management held a hearing on security and privacy impacts on the use of drones in the United States".

Legislation is destined to define airspace related to drones and most likely how they can be utilized by the general public. For private investigators, drones will have to follow previous cases laws and you therefore will not be able to hover above a person's yard where there is an expectation of privacy. The issue of trespass and

---

[20] http://www.nciss.org/

invasion of privacy is sure to be among the issues raised by the use of drones.

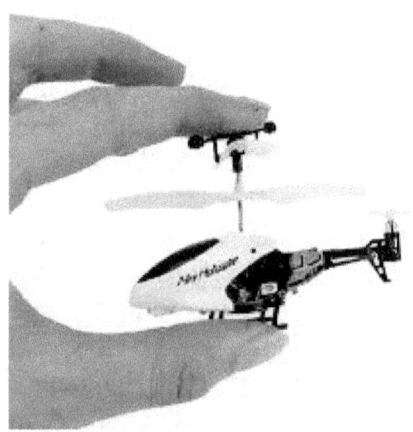

Example of Drones

INTERNATIONAL SURVEILLANCE
Chapter Sixteen

Once the investigator has grown good at doing surveillance in their local area, being able to do so in another part of the state of the other end of the U.S. can often confuse a PI since they are out of their element. Those that can do so in different parts of the United States sometimes can adapt their talents and do cases outside of the United States. Unless you have traveled some internationally, you will be in for a tremendous amount of operational and cultural obstacles and learning these at the expense of your client is not recommended.

It is highly recommended that if you do decide to make the trip yourself, having a local PI to assist is an absolute. First, they will be licensed so this will take care of most legal concerns. The local PI will also have a good grasp of the culture, geographic area, traffic issues, construction related concerns and should have good contacts with law enforcement. The fact that you talk with a different dialect and have physical characteristics that are different from people in the particular country also makes you stand out more. The clothes that Americans wear will usually demonstrate differences as well.

Other issues that many do not think of include recharging equipment. Most countries operate on a different type of electrical current such as PAL, have different receptacles and may damage your equipment.

Sometimes just knowing how to navigate Customs and Immigration can be important. If you are going into another country to do surveillance, rarely should you ever tell anyone that you are entering the country to work. I teach scuba diving as a hobby and am a Dive Master. There are lakes, rivers and oceans everywhere so I always carry my scuba card with me and that is my cover. In some countries, you have to have a special visa to work or you may have to be sponsored by a national. My personal preference is to go in low-key, under the radar. I get the job done and get out before anyone knows I was even there.

Many countries are adverse towards the United States in general and the mere fact that you are an American can create hazards. Anyone anticipating travel abroad should check with the U.S. government's Department of State [21] to determine any travel warnings or other useful information about the country. The PI should also make an effort to learn about the country they will be entering. Simple internet searches can accomplish much of this but you should learn as much about the culture as possible. I have always used a travel agent as they are connected to the travel industry and often can provide very useful information. They agent can also assist in helping find hotels that are friendly to Americans and well as safe.

When traveling abroad, you should only drink bottled water and bottled beverages as the local water may have contaminants that will make a non-local sick. You should also not eat anything washed in local water (lettuce, etc…) that is not cooked as washing food in the same water you refuse to drink will end in the same resulting sickness. You choice of floors in the hotel is also important as many countries are poor and do not have proper fire-fighting equipment. Many have fire trucks with ladders that will not reach beyond 7-8 floors. Staying on the lower levels will help not only for this reason but in case you need to flee the hotel area quickly.

Getting out of the country is more important than getting in. I recommend that you take the time to study the region to understand what countries border the country you will be entering. Get a detailed map of the city/state/country and study it. Forward it to an email such as Yahoo or similar that you can access anywhere in the world. Have a plan on which direction you will travel, which country you would get to that is nearby and friendly to Americans. Exchange money ahead of time at your bank (lower rates) or at airport kiosks and insure that you have local currency available.

Traveling abroad with a clumsy laptop or similar device is not recommended. Many countries will "check" your computer and

---

[21] http://travel.state.gov/travel/cis_pa_tw/cis_pa_tw_1168.html

make a copy of the hard-drive while you are being "processed" through Customs and Immigration. Any documents you need should be kept on an encrypted USB thumb-drive or similar device. Your cell phone will most likely be useless unless you contacted your provider ahead of time and made arrangements for use out of the country. This will be expensive and even so, may not work in the other country. Purchase calling cards once you reach the airport where you enter the country. You may also be able to rent a cell phone locally or purchase a throw-away phone that you can load pre-paid phone cards on and restock as required. Any of this is subject to being lost, stolen or hacked so scrutinize what you need to take, how you communicate and what is absolutely necessary to transmit.

You should check the area for the possibility of natural disasters from earthquakes, volcanoes and other related unforeseen problems. Prior to traveling abroad you should also contact your doctor to determine what vaccines are required and/or recommended for the region you will be traveling. You should check to make sure you have a passport that is valid with at least 6 months before having to be renewed, check for any visas needed to enter the country and makes copies and keep in your luggage as well as leaving copies with loved ones and at your office. In the event your passport is stolen this will help speed the ability to obtain a new one.

Often your insurance will not cover you in other countries. If you get sick or injured abroad, you may have to pay any medical bills before being allowed to leave the country. I recommend paying for the services of Med jet[22] as they will send a fully staffed medical airplane to get you back into a medical facility in the U.S. The cost is as low as $99 to be a member and receive coverage. Having traveled to the vast majority of continents and countries, important information like this is priceless.

The general overall tone regarding other countries is that they are not as liberal with their privacy laws as in the United States. In many countries information is only available through an attorney who does much more tasks that are not directly associated with attorneys such as notary services. They will conduct the research

---

[22] http://medjetassist.com/

and "notarize" the documents to make them legal to give to a third party. Many private investigators in foreign countries actually operate under the umbrella of security guard services or consultants.

The following is a snapshot of some countries and their licensing requirements. Much of this was compiled from PI's that I know all over the world and comes directly from those that are actually performing private investigations.

Africa

North Africa: Egypt, Morocco. No legal status and PI's operate with consultants and security officers.

East Africa: Somalia, Tanzania, Uganda, Kenya, Rwanda

No legal status and PI's operate with consultants, lawyers and security officers.

Australia

Australia has six states and two territories and each have their own licensing requirements. A PI must complete a Certificate 111 course in investigations from PRS03 Asset Security Training Package approved by the Australian National Training Authority Act of 1992. The Commonwealth Privacy Act of 1982 prohibits PI's from accessing much of the personal information on individuals and requires that PI's take reasonable steps to give individuals notice of any inquiries.

Australia – Victoria[23]

The private security industry encompasses a broad range of activities including security guarding, crowd controllers, investigators, bodyguards, private security trainers, security advisors and equipment installers. The Private Security Act 2004

---

[23] http://www.police.vic.gov.au/content.asp?Document_ID=109

was enacted to preserve the safety and peace of all Victorians with regards to private security.

Any person or business undertaking private security activities in the State of Victoria must be the holder of a Private Security License or Registration issued by Victoria Police.

The private security industry is regulated by Victoria Police's Licensing & Regulation Division (LRD).

LRD is responsible for:

- Granting private security licenses and registrations, including renewals
- Approval of training and trainers
- Compliance and enforcement activities

Australia – New South Wales[24]

Private investigators in New South Wales are regulated under the Commercial Agents and Private Inquiry Agents Act 2004.

Australia – South Australia[25]

Private investigators are required to be licensed by the Security and Investigation Agents Act 1995 - SECT **6**

6—Obligation to be licensed

(1) A person must not—

(a) carry on business, or otherwise act, as a security agent or investigation agent except as authorized by a license under this Part; or

(b) advertise or otherwise hold himself or herself out as being entitled to carry on business, or to otherwise act, as a security agent or investigation agent unless authorized to so act by a license under this Part.

Maximum penalty: $20 000.

---

[24] http://www.austlii.edu.au/au/legis/nsw/consol_act/caapiaa2004429/
[25] http://www.austlii.edu.au/au/legis/sa/consol_act/saiaa1995360/s6.html

Australia – Western Australia[26]

Private investigators are required to be licensed under the Security and Related Activities (Control) Act 1996.

Australia – Tasmania[27]

Private investigators are required to be licensed under the Security and Investigations Agents Act 2002.

Canada

In Canada all licensing is provincial. Each province breaks it down similar but different with most licenses being security guard, private investigator and security consultant.

The usual requirements are over 19, no criminal record, Canadian citizen and in that case you get a "under supervision" license. With appropriate military law enforcement experience you can have the under supervision removed. Otherwise it is typically 2000 hours required along with whatever that province may require. No guns are allowed for any of those licenses. Some provinces do allow the use of handcuffs or restraints if you pass another course that trains you in the use of them.

Recently a couple of Provinces including Ontario enacted a mandatory 40 hour basic course for licensing followed by an exam. Existing licences were exempt from the 40 hour course but, not the exam.

---

[26] http://www.slp.wa.gov.au/statutes/swans.nsf/f0c1172198578b78c82573ed001b6aae/2fe8c409103fba4f4825702a00140abe?OpenDocument

[27] http://www.thelaw.tas.gov.au/tocview/index.w3p;cond=;doc_id=19%2B%2B2002%2BGS3%40EN%2B20060101000000;histon=;prompt=;rec=;term

<u>China</u>

Individuals conducting investigations in China do not have to have a license although the PI profession is not recognized and highly scrutinized. Most operate under a consultant's title.

<u>Costa Rica</u> No licensing.

<u>Europe – General Licensing</u>[28]

Out of 38 states, 20 countries have legal requirements regarding PI licensing. There are 7 countries in the drafting stages, 8 with no requirements and 3 with unclear or conflicting information. The same general requirements are included regarding minimum age, clear criminal history, minimum experience and proof of competence.

---

[28] International Federation of Associations of Private Detectives

Legal regulations for PI's (1)

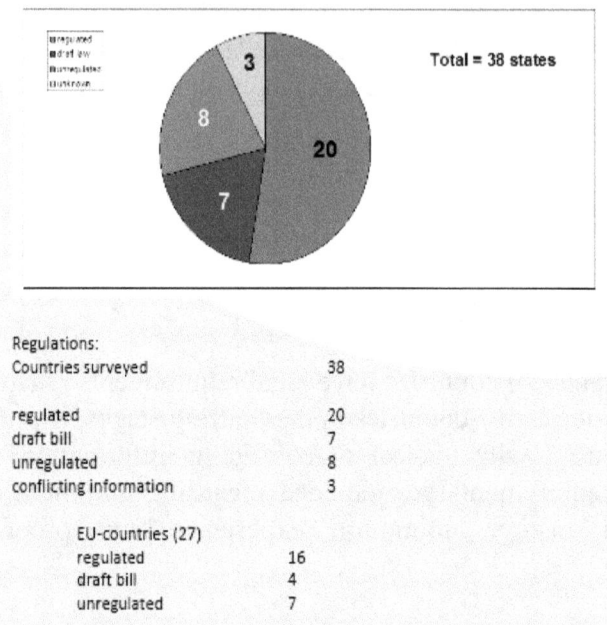

Regulations:
Countries surveyed 38

regulated 20
draft bill 7
unregulated 8
conflicting information 3

EU-countries (27)
regulated 16
draft bill 4
unregulated 7

Finland

In Finland the security industry is regulated by "Law on Private Security Services" which came into effect in 2002. The law is currently under reform and the renewed legislation should come into force in 2013 or 2014.

There is a distinction however, as only Private Investigators who aim to expose crimes have to be licensed. The "private investigator" as a professional title is not protected in Finland. Thus, anybody can call themselves private investigator, and for example locate people, or conduct background checks and infidelity investigations, as long as the aim of the investigation is not to expose crimes.

Private investigators who *professionally conduct operations with the aim to expose crimes* are required to be licensed by the police authorities. Also, *individuals and companies involved in security guard operations or personal protection are required to have a license*. The license requirements for an individual are: 18 years of age, honesty and dependability and suitability of personal characteristics, not restricted capacity to act, sufficient assets; and for a company: sufficient assets, the responsible persons need to meet the requirements for an individual.

It should be noted that private investigator as a professional title is not protected in Finland. Thus, anybody can call themselves private investigator, and for example locate people, or conduct background checks and infidelity investigations, as long as the aim of the investigation is not to expose crimes.

Germany

In Germany no license is required. We do Process-Service with or without affidavit. If an affidavit is needed we use our Notary law-office.

Greece

Greece requires PI's to be licensed but personal information is highly protected by the Personal Data Protection law. Much of the background information has to be obtained through associations with paralegals/lawyers. As for surveillance, it is allowed as long as it is conducted in public places and not in private property areas.

Hungary

PIs in Hungary need only general (national) license issued by the local police. We can do:

1. Surveillance
2. Due diligence
3. Background check
4. Educational check
5. FCPA research

Prohibited due to the very strict Hungarian privacy law:

1. Phone tapping

2. Criminal record check

Not prohibited but almost impossible without candidate's written permission include doing a credit check, litigation or business disputes on record. Unfortunately there is no public central databank for litigation here.

India

There are no licensing requirements for PI's. However, privacy laws are very strict and you cannot conduct or issue a report on a subject without their written permission.

Indonesia

Companies conducting private investigations must be licensed with the Indonesian National Police although individuals are not required to have a license but must work under a licensed company. Individuals can receive training from police and receive a certificate.

Israel

A license is required and is issued by the Ministry of Justice and renewed every year. There are four levels of licensing:
-Trainee.
-Single PI
-Union of PIs
-Management of investigations firm
A special committee headed by a district judge controls legal aspects of the profession.

Italy

Italy is a State with many regions and the Interior Office has a Prefect in each main town and is empowered to release the PI license. The applicant must meet requirements including education, training, experience, citizenship, etc...) There are two types of PI licenses including one for civil felonies, private disputes, etc... and the other one for penal crimes (this requires more features and experience in that specific field). Some PIs can obtain both. The license must be renewed each year and the PI is obliged to register each operation as soon as he receives the mandate from the client. The license is a national license and the Italian State Police can come any time to inspect the office.

Japan

There is no requirement for an individual to be licensed as a private investigator. However, they do have to be on record with the Prefectural Police Department and must undergo an annual audit based on the Act of Regulation on Private Detectives Services (2003).

Kazakhstan, Kyrgyzstan, Uzbekistan, Azerbaijan

There is no legal status, though security industry is legalized. We expect legislation changes. PI's operate using lawyers consultants and security officers.

Korea

Private Investigators do have to be licensed and are overseen by the Korean National Police.

Malaysia

PI's must be licensed by the Ministry of Home Affairs and obtain a private detective license.

Middle East Arab Countries

PIs are not recognized as a legal profession. PI's operate utilizing lawyers, consultants and security officers.

Mongolia

No legal status and PI's operate via lawyers and consultants.

Nepal

No legal status and PI's operate as consultants.

New Zealand

PI's do have to be licensed and is regulated under the Private Security Personnel and Private Investigators Act of 2010 by the Private Security Personnel Licensing Authority.

Nigeria:

In Nigeria, private detectives business is prohibited by Law – (Private Guards Act 1990). Only lawyers and regulated accountants who must be working for one employer are exempted. Anyone who claims to be licensed in this country is operating illegally.

Pakistan

Private Investigators do have to obtain a PI license but companies currently are not give a license, only the PI.

Philippines

Private Investigators do have to be licensed and are overseen by the Philippine National Police.

Russia

PI license is required issued by Ministry of Internal Affairs. Police can object issuing a license.

Singapore

All companies in Singapore must be registered with the Accounting and Corporate Authority of Singapore to conduct and operate a business in Singapore. They can be sole proprietorships, partnerships or a private limited company. The security industry in

Singapore is fairly small and the investigations fraternity, which comes under the banner of the security industry is even smaller. There are approximately 275 security agencies in Singapore with about 120 agencies that also running the investigations business.

All security and investigations firms in Singapore must be licensed by the Singapore Police. In the past, they are being licensed by the Criminal Investigations Department and every person who serves as a security officer and/or investigator must get a clearance before they can work. The license however, is given to the company and they are bound by the Private Security and Investigations Agency Act (amended on 27 April 2009). The company must have a Licensee who is the Managing Director of the company. Eligibility includes police or military background (leadership position – that is from sergeant onwards), "0" level education. Today, licensee must also attend mandatory training. Only Singaporeans and Malaysians (limited quota per company) are eligible. No other foreigners are permitted to work as security officers or investigators even till today!

Sri Lanka

Private investigators do have to be licensed by the Civil Division of Ministry of Defense and Colombo Divisional Secretariat.

Thailand

Private investigators are required to be licensed

Taiwan

Private investigations are regulated. Personal privacy laws do not allow almost any public records on people or companies and that legal action is mainly criminal due to the nature of Taiwan civil and criminal laws.

United Kingdom

Currently the PI profession is unlicensed, however, this will change in 2014 and PI's will be under the Security Industry Authority

Vietnam

Security guards have to be licensed but commercial investigations are not allowed in Vietnam. Market research and consulting is permitted.

ABOUT THE AUTHOR
Chapter Seventeen

Professional Experience Narrative: Mr. Riddle has more than 35 years of investigative experience and earned a Bachelor of Science degree in Criminal Justice from the University of North Alabama. He was chosen as the **"PI of the Year"** by the National Association of Investigative Specialists and the PI Magazine named Mr. Riddle as the **"#1 PI in the United States"**. He has been designated an expert in surveillance, insurance investigations, nursing home abuse and computer investigations. He was chosen as **"One of the Top 25 PI's of the 20th Century."** Kelly obtained his **Texas Certified Investigator** designation (less than 50 in TX.) Mr. Riddle is also the past **President (2010-2012) for TALI** - the Texas Association of Licensed Investigators (TALI); **Board of Directors (2007-2010) for TALI** as well as being on the Board of Directors for the **Freedom of Information Foundation of Texas**. Kelly is on the Public Relations committee for the **Council of International Investigators** and the Membership Chair for the San Antonio Chapter of ASIS. He is a Founding Board Member and Board Advisor for the non-profit organization "Can You Identify Me." Kelly was the recipient of the **2013 Hudgins-Sallee award**, the highest recognition presented by the Texas Association of Licensed Investigators.

Mr. Riddle is the author of 10 books and has published more than 40 articles. He has been the guest speaker at more than 400 events and has been on national TV, radio and newspapers.

Prior law enforcement experience includes being a member of the SWAT team, a Training Officer, Emergency Medical Technician, Evidence Technician, Arson Investigator, Juvenile Specialist and Traffic Investigator.

Mr. Riddle is the Founder and President of the **PI Institute of Education**, as well as the **Association of Christian Investigators** with more than 1000 members in the U.S. and 19 countries. Kelly is the Founder of the **Coalition of Association Leaders** comprised of past and present board members from state, national and international associations.

Mr. Riddle is a member of NAIS,TALI,ASIS,NALI,FAPI,LAPI, USAPI,ACI, NAAA,PICA,WIN, NLLI, CTIB, CLEAR,IOPIA,TIDA,CII,ASSIST

For more information, please review our websites at www.kelmarpi.com, www.a-c-i.com and www.PIinstitute.com. You may reach Mr. Riddle via the Internet at the e-mail address of Kelly@KelmarGlobal.com.

Kelly E. Riddle

Index

Access Road Surveillance	page 57
Child Welfare Cases	page 70
Community Property	page 149
Criss-cross pattern	page 59
Curb Technique	page 49
Electronic Frontier Foundation	page 152
Expressway Surveillance	page 56
Intersection Use for Surveillance	page 76
NCISS	page 153
Pinnacle Studio Software	page 17
Police Contact	page 88
Rules of Evidence	page 109
Seven Prong Test	page 110
Street-over Technique	page 12
Sony DVD burner	page 17
Squeeze Technique	page 139
Surveillance definition	page 4
TALI Survey	page 120
Turn-off technique	page 63
Unmanned Aircraft Systems	page 151
U.S. –v- Jones	page 150